AF483639

My Journey into Wholeness
from Trauma to Healing

An art journal

by Mary Emma Jones, Ph.D.

ISBN-13: 979-8-218-12907-1

Printed and bound in the United States of America.

I dedicate this book to my family.

You have always been there for me,
creating a safe haven for laughter, tears, joy, and challenging conversations
that enlarge and enlighten my world.

To each one of you:
To my husband and my partner in this life, Robin
To my daughter and my very dear friend, Darcy
And to my son and my storyteller, Sam.

I am so deeply grateful.

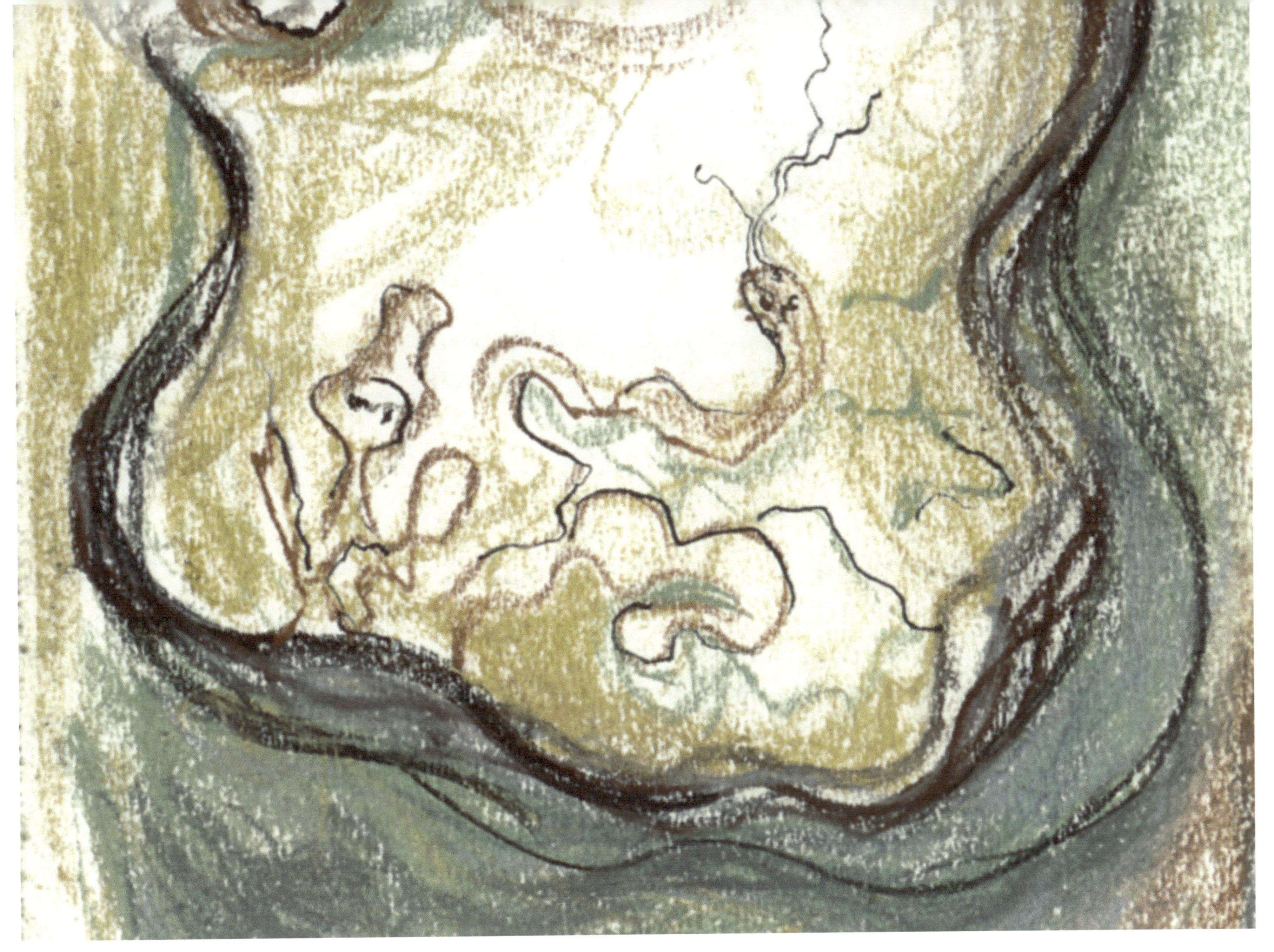

Deep underground, there were stirrings ...

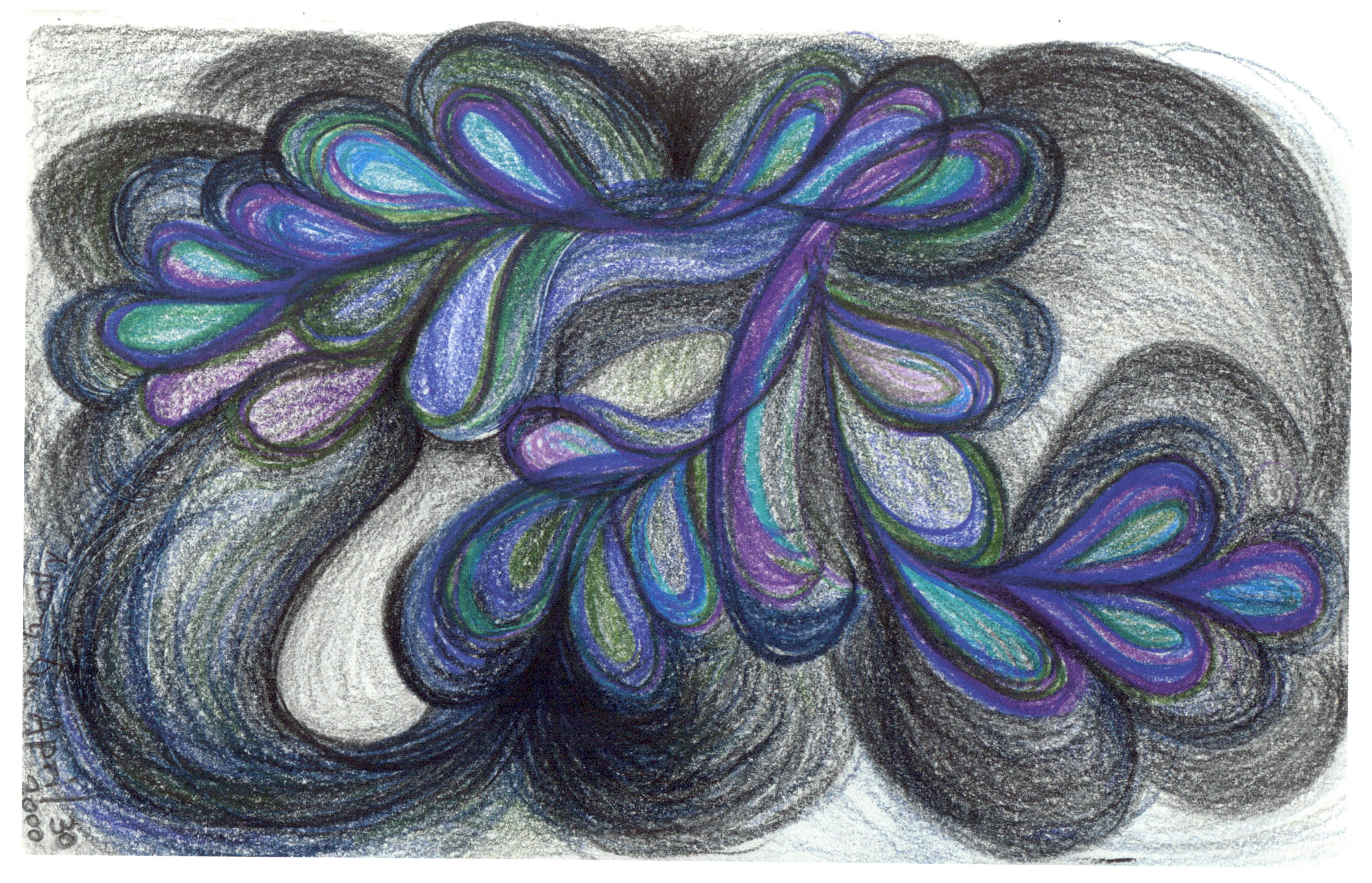

... of bubbling color

No Words

No words
They are not needed today
They do not belong here yet.

What are these bubbles of light
Emerging from darkness and confusion
Exploding from the jaws of death
What darkness is it that contains such light

For now there are no words.

May 7, 2000

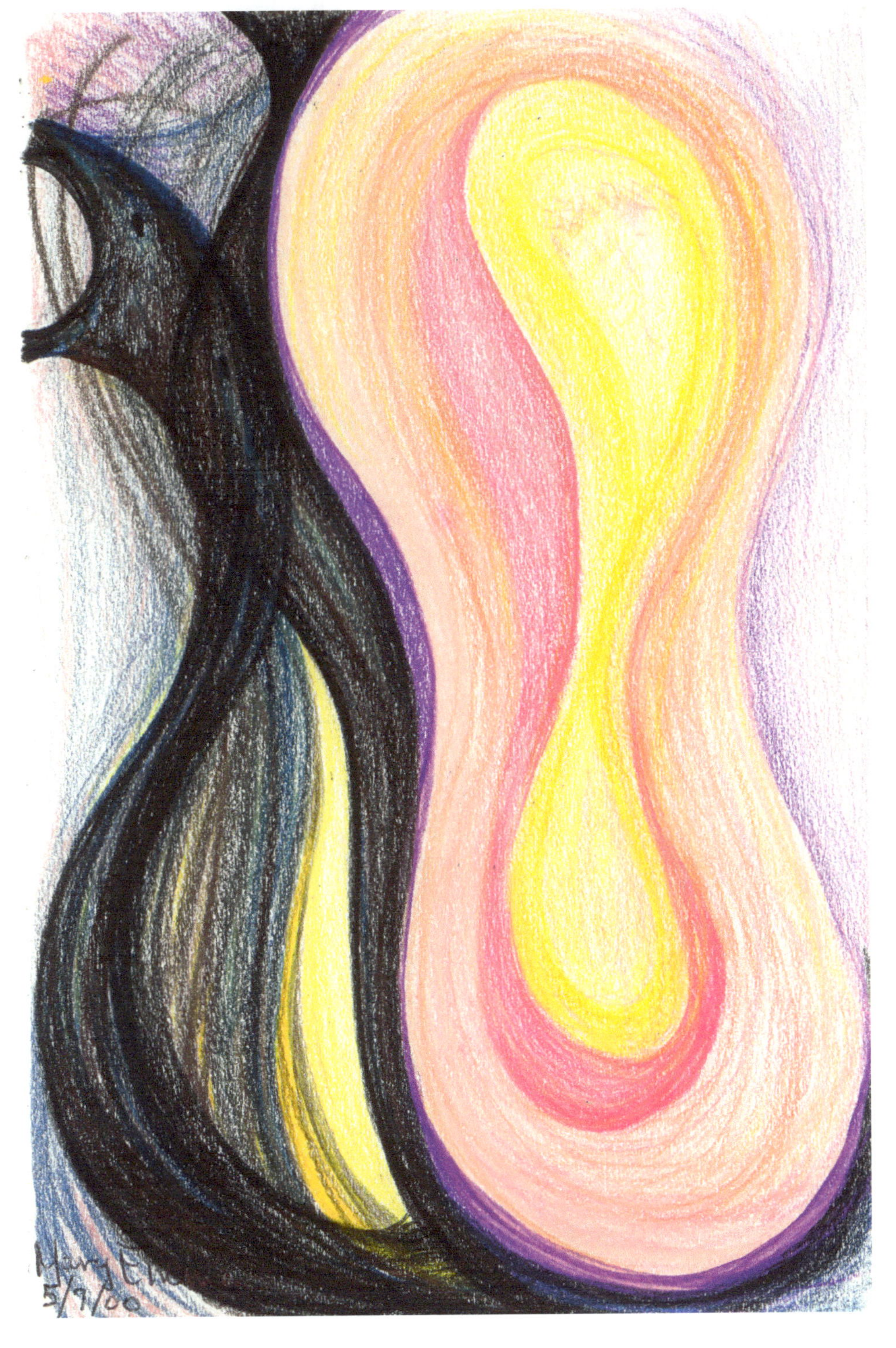

This story began a very long time ago.

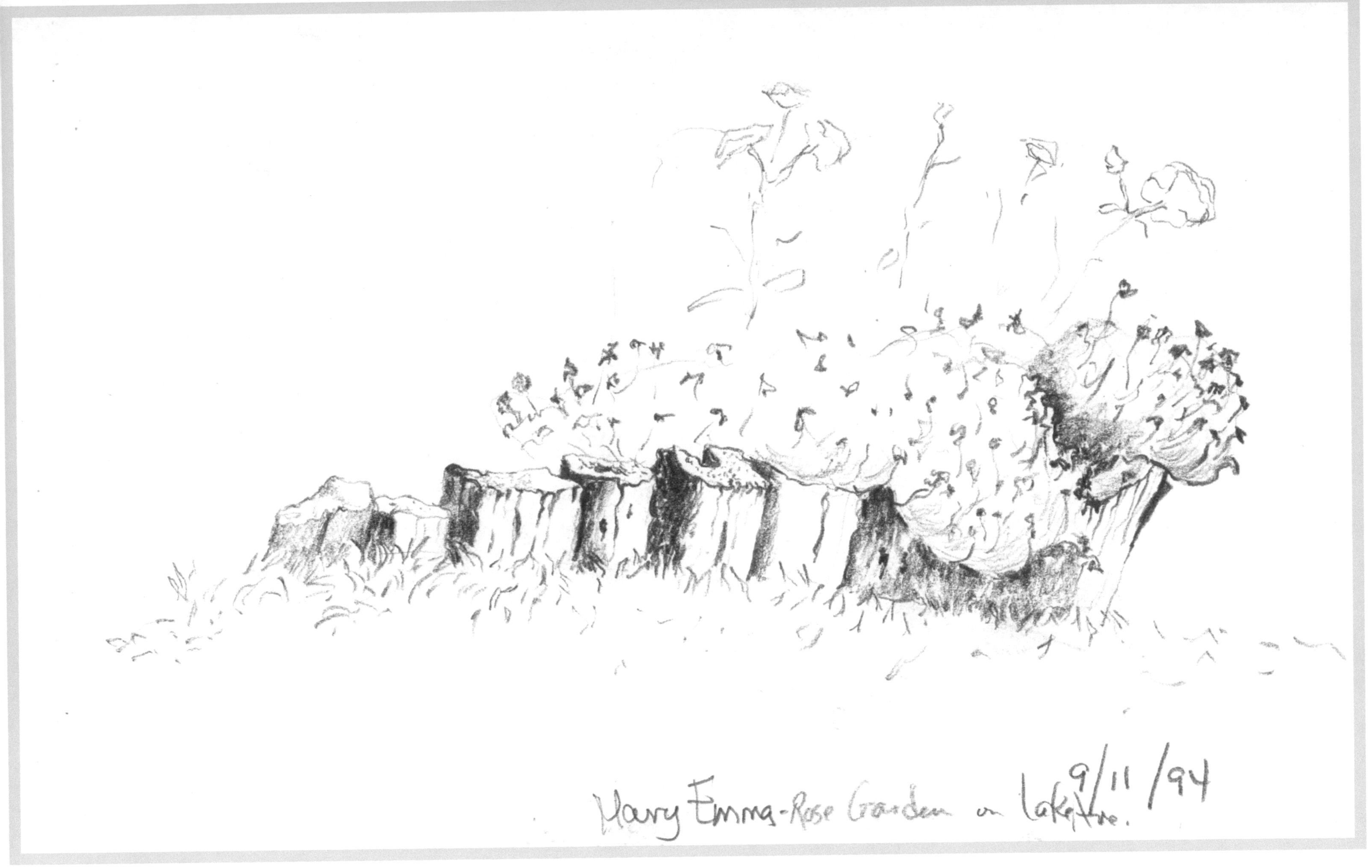

One day on a walk down Lake Avenue, she saw a beautiful park where the flowers of late summer were still blooming.

Plant Woman

I go to that place where
Color and shape and tears
Arise to tell my story.
The story is a mystery still.
I find clarity in line and shape.
A space opens

For color

For tears

For terror

For joy

So who are you?
Some kind of Plant Woman.

Vibrating

Dancing

Blooming Creature
Who somehow seems so familiar
I love you!

October 21, 2011

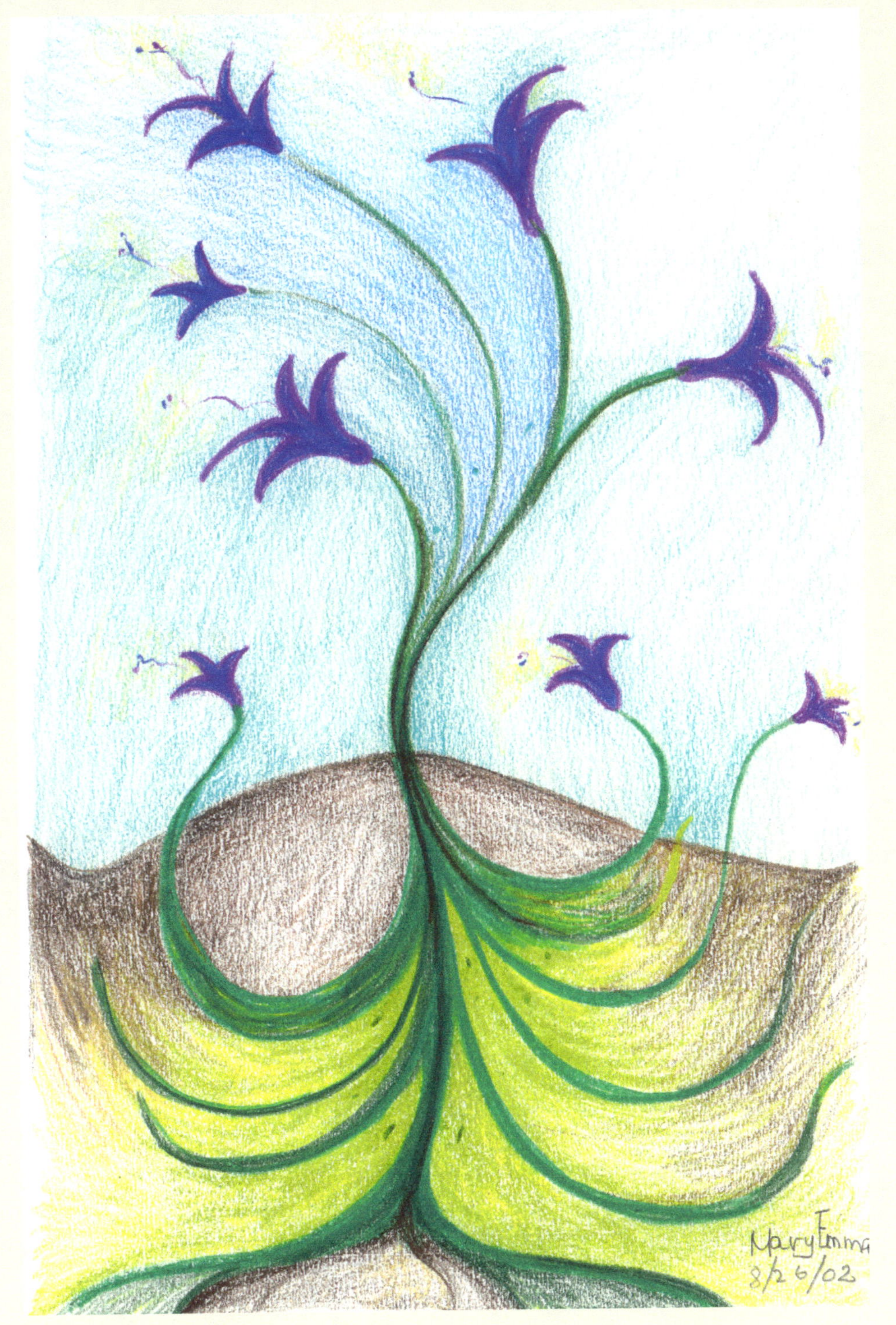

Mary Emma
8/2 6/02

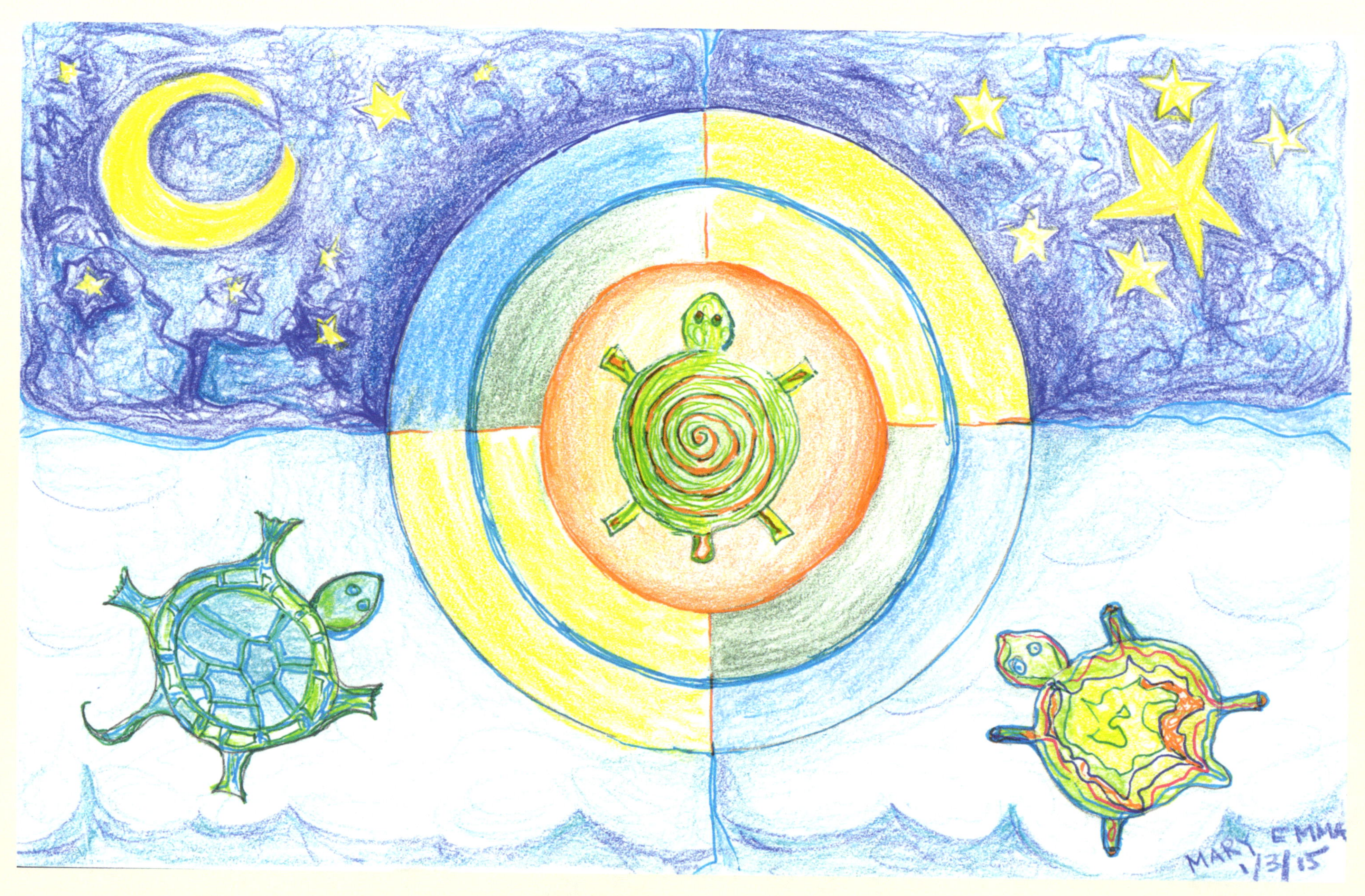

We are safe, connected, and free.

So...where does a doodle begin? a mandala doodle? I think it
must begin with a circle, a nicely drawn circle using an
old Turkish ashtray that most likely belonged to my father.
Oops...my mind just left me. Where did it go? To hidden
memories of my father's blue eyes?

So I ask you again. Where does a doodle, a mandala
doodle, begin. Deep, I think, inside the psyche, from a
tight little knot that begins sending messages in color and
shape to the edges...and beyond. Reaching out through
space and time.

Blooming on the inside,

Blooming on the outside.

I'm coming as fast as I can!

Two birds, still there waiting.

January 4, 2016

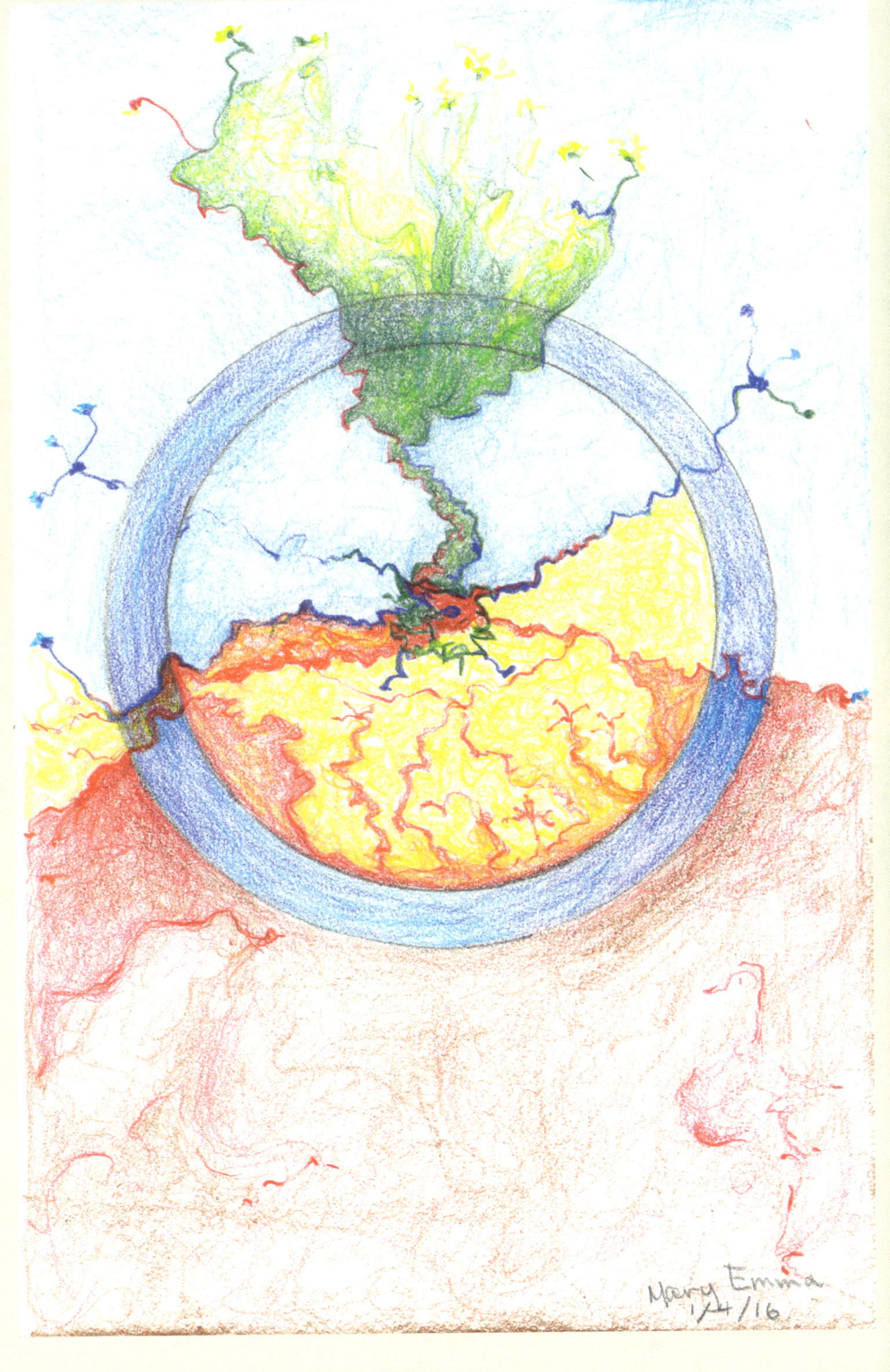

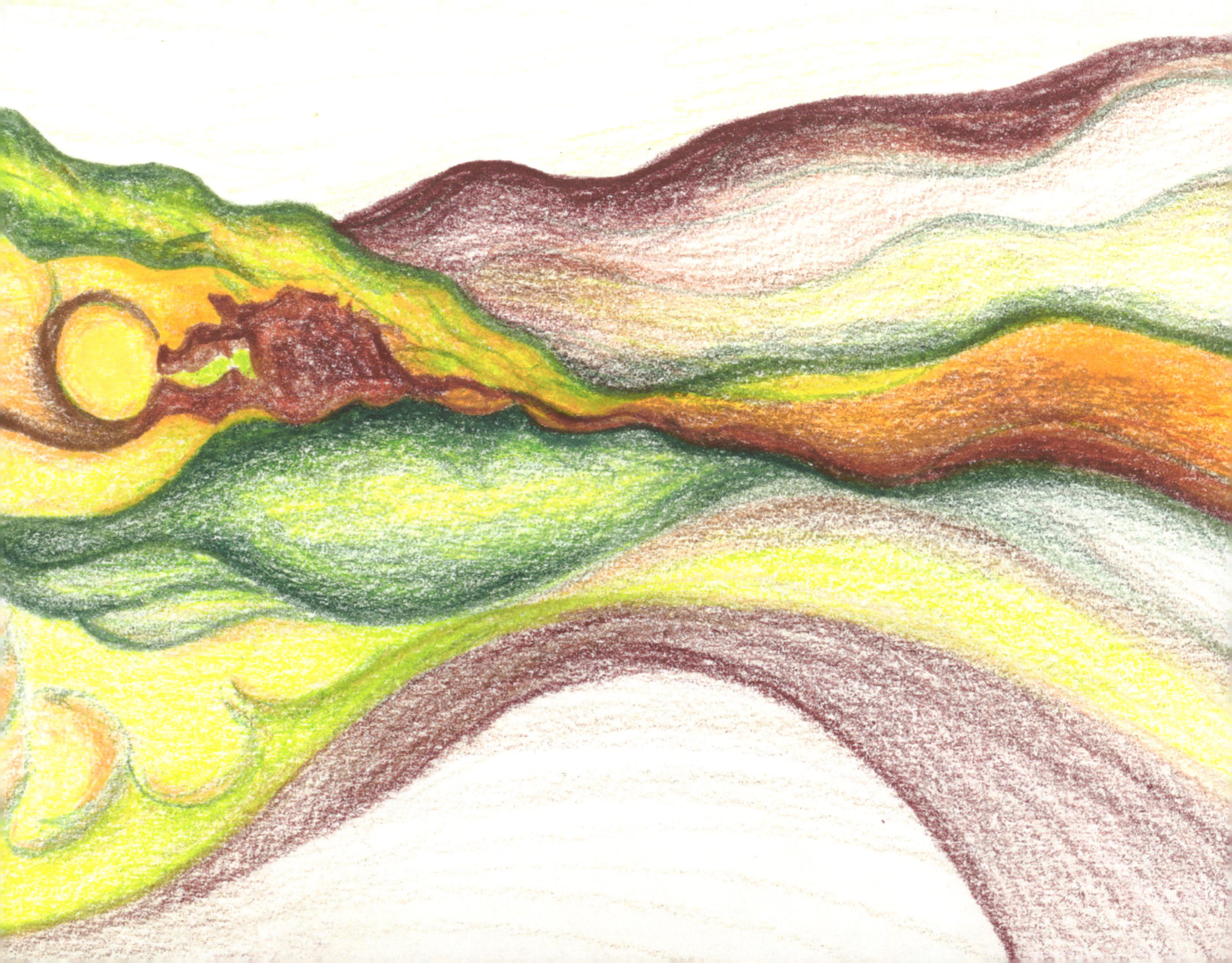

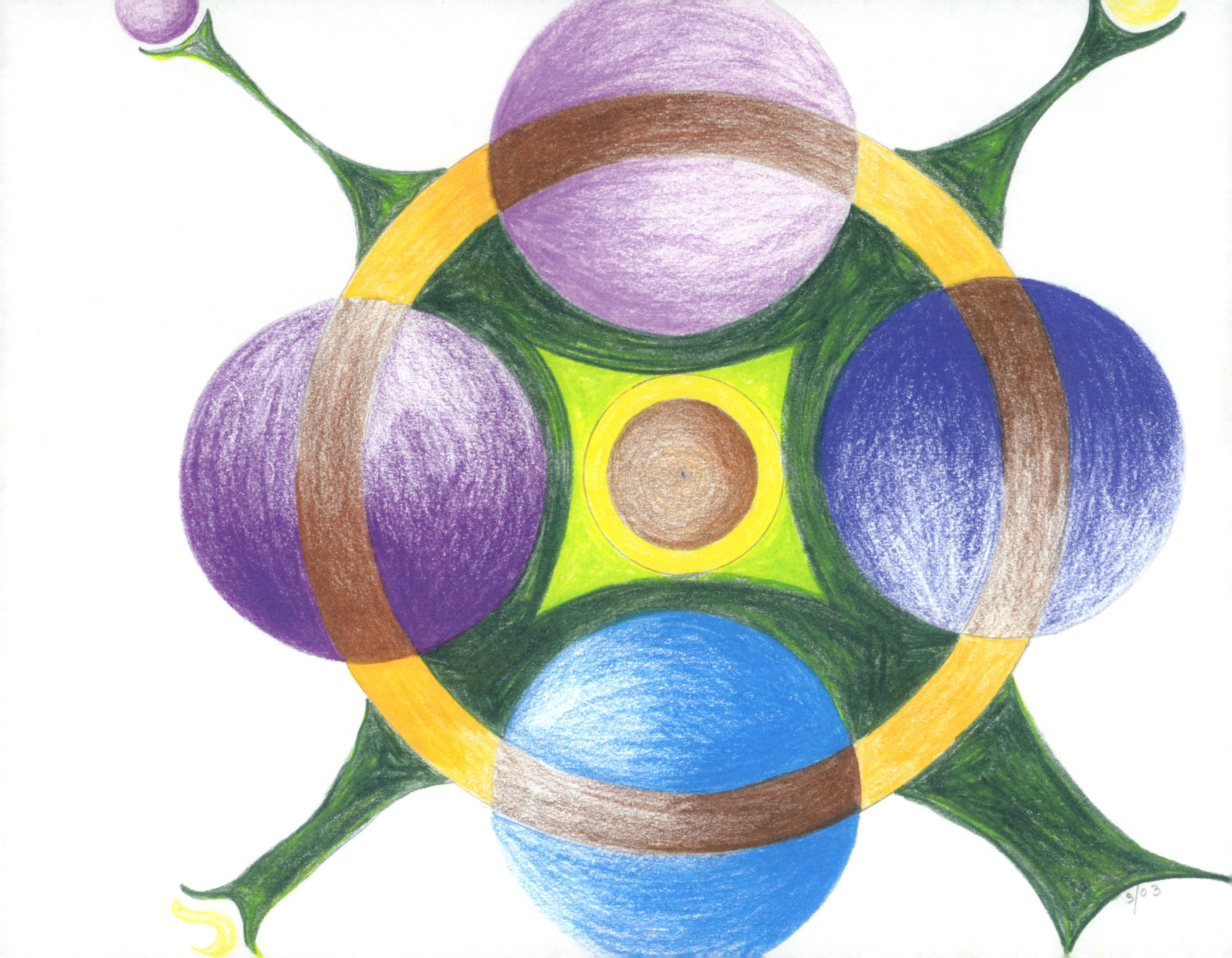

Excerpt from My Memoirs: A Case Study
Mary Emma Brown Jones, Ph.D.
July 31, 2021
During the Pandemic

I still don't know exactly how it happened. It was like I had lost myself in the chaos of my life, a life that I had worked very hard to organize so I could work as a psychologist in Blairsville, Georgia. Following my doctoral program at The University of Georgia, I returned to my home near Blairsville to establish a private practice as a psychologist with a dear friend and colleague. We established our practice in the two-story building overlooking the golf course just north of town. We loved it there. Our offices were on either side of an ample and well-lit waiting room filled with a kids' corner and healing pictures on the walls.

In March 2020, the coronavirus started showing up in the news with dire warnings about its danger. I decided very quickly to move my practice to my house, which I share with my husband, Robin, at the foot of Brasstown Bald Mountain, tucked in a cove surrounded by the horseshoe-shaped mountain range. I transformed my practice from seeing clients at my office in Blairsville to a space upstairs in my studio, where I met with clients via a video platform. I am realizing now how disruptive that move was. I was so happy working in my upstairs office overlooking the golf course. I was not ready to move; neither was my colleague and good friend. We had almost no time to think about or process that move.

In the meantime, the pandemic got worse and worse. Robin and I finally got our Moderna vaccines in February 2021, when Covid deaths in the U.S. had reached approximately 630,000. We must have been relieved and excited because we planned a vacation to Hilton Head almost immediately. That March, we spent a week on the north end of the island in an apartment, part of a large complex, right on Port Royal Sound. I found myself trying to orient to normal, whatever that might look like. In March, I must have thought that meant doing things I had missed out on in a year of Covid. I then decided that I could begin seeing clients in person, so Robin and I began the task of cleaning and organizing our basement, a huge and overwhelming task. The basement was where Robin had brought the tools he had accumulated over his decades of housebuilding and movie work. We created a cozy psychology office that would help clients feel comfortable and safe.

About the end of April 2021, I got a persistent dry cough and severe sore throat. I wondered if it was Covid, so I got tested. It was not. I was mentally and physically exhausted. So today, I am looking back to see if I can figure out how I got here, to a place in my mind that seems so lost. I am trying to find the pieces of myself that had scattered during the pandemic and the earlier traumas of my life.

Thursday, December 24, 2020:

I began doing "morning pages" in 1993, when I was working with my dissertation consultant. She was a supportive woman during this difficult time as I was writing my dissertation. She told me about the book The Artist's Way by Julia Cameron, and I have been doing "morning pages" on and off since that time. In some ways, I feel I have lost my way again, so I am hoping that these morning pages will once more help me find my authentic path. Perhaps my issue is this Covid pandemic! It came so suddenly upon me, upon all of us, wrenching us from our moorings, our jobs, our social connections, our ways of thinking about the world.

Saturday, December 26, 2020:

Morning pages help me stay in the present moment. There was a time when I did not know about the present moment as a clinical concept and yet I would find myself absorbed in something I was doing—a hobby, a drawing, a book. As a child, I loved to read. I still do. And when I am reading, I feel fully present with the story. As a child, growing up in the country on our farm along the Little River in Middle Georgia, I used to love spending time in the woods exploring and playing with my brother and our neighbor boys. We would play Cowboys and Indians for hours and hours, forgetting about time as we enacted the stories we made up as we went along. I used to love dressing up as Davy Crockett or his son, and exploring the woods alone inside the story I had made up for that day. I also loved creating scrapbooks and getting fully absorbed in the story I was telling about certain events in my life.

I want to do that now... write, draw, color, paint, make scrapbooks, and go on adventures. The book you are holding is the way I have come to understand the confusion of the pandemic and the events of my life—so that I can come to integrate those pieces of myself in this present moment.

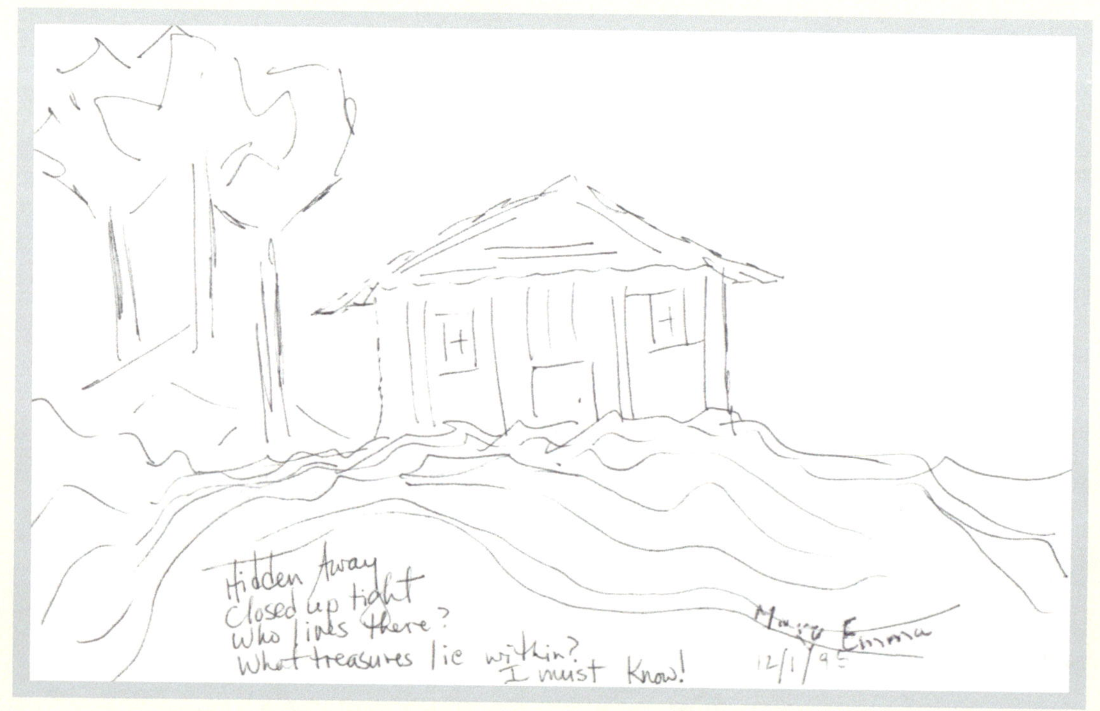

Hidden away
Closed up tight
Who lives there?
What treasures lie within?
I must know!

As I prepare this book, I know that my own story is couched within the stories of women all over the world.

In the midst of a passionate conversation among friends at a conference years ago, we declared that it was time for women to come more fully into our own power and make decisions for ourselves.

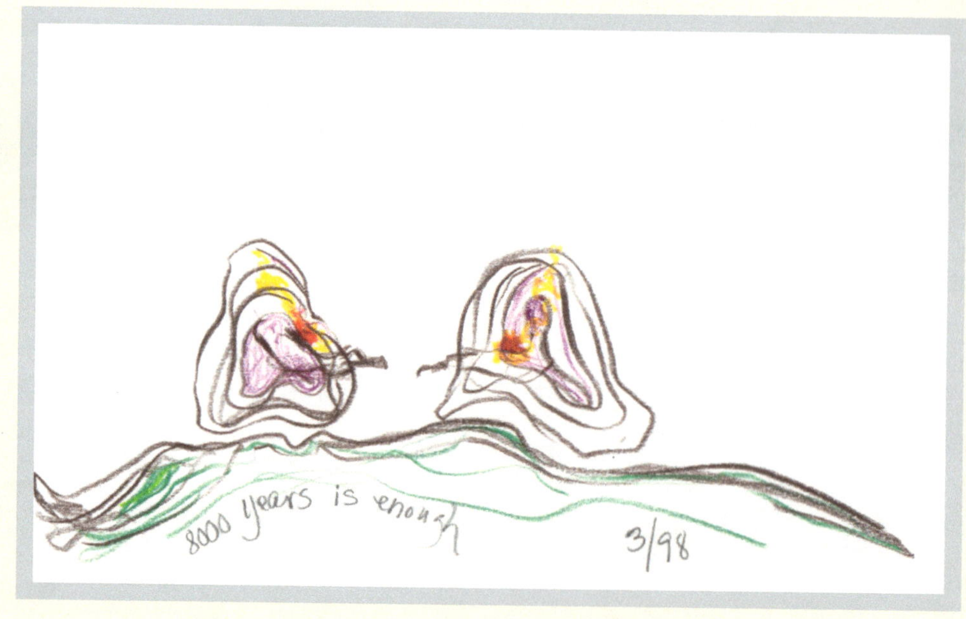

My body ... my mud
You have held me
  Cradled
    Trapped
     Protected
For so long ...
I ask for release
and yet you choose to hold me ...
Hidden in the depths of your safety
    I am waiting for the dance.

Will you join me?

August 21, 1999

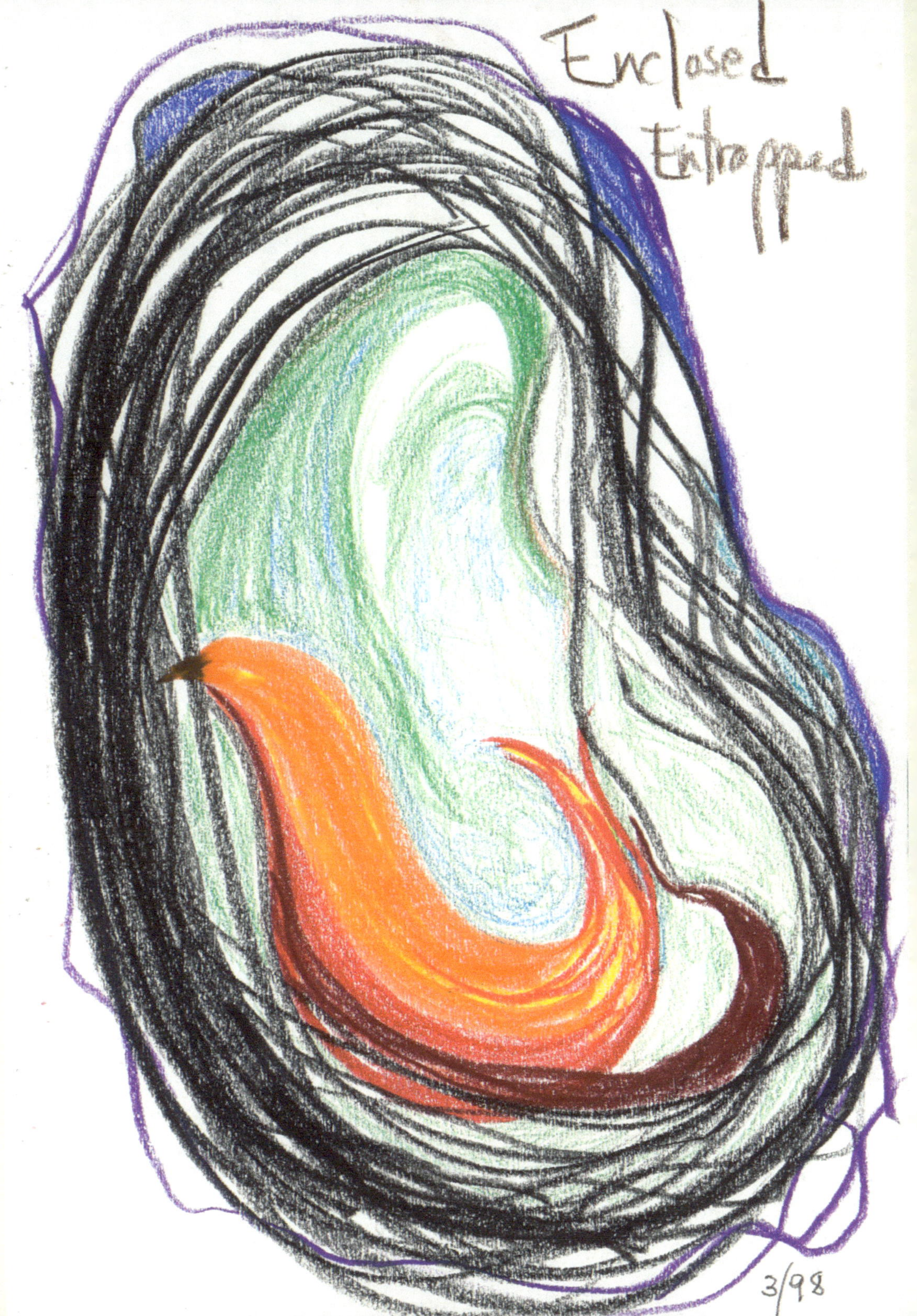

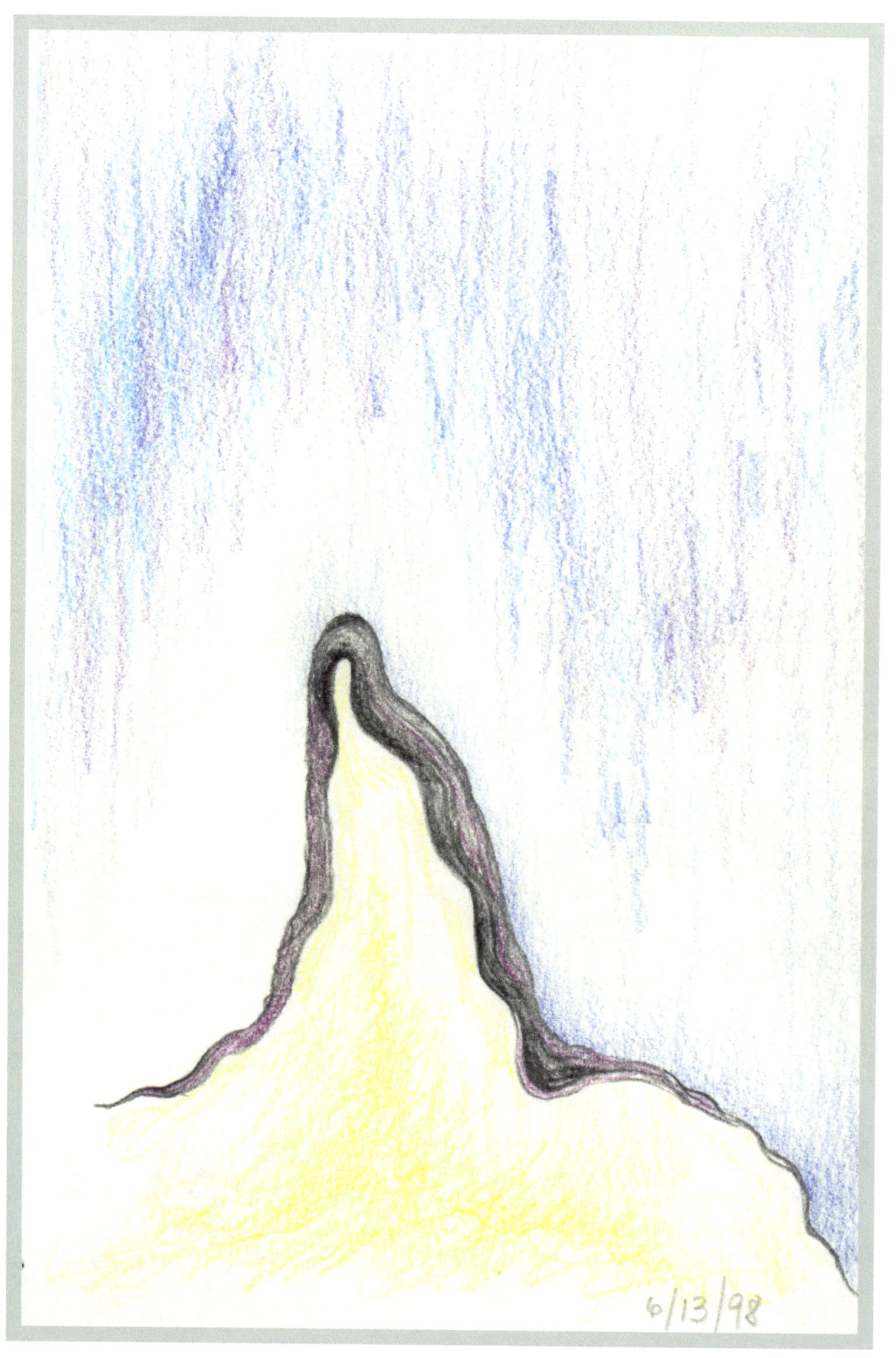

6/13/98

I don't like being so lonely
My body feels so heavy and I hurt
My arms and legs feel like lead and my face muscles droop.

Where is my smile?
Where is my excitement?
Where is my passion?
Where is my enthusiasm?
They are all gone now
I miss you!
   I miss your arms that hold me close to you
   I miss your eyes that see mine so deeply
   I miss how I feel when you are here
   I miss the me that I am when you are near.

June 13, 1998

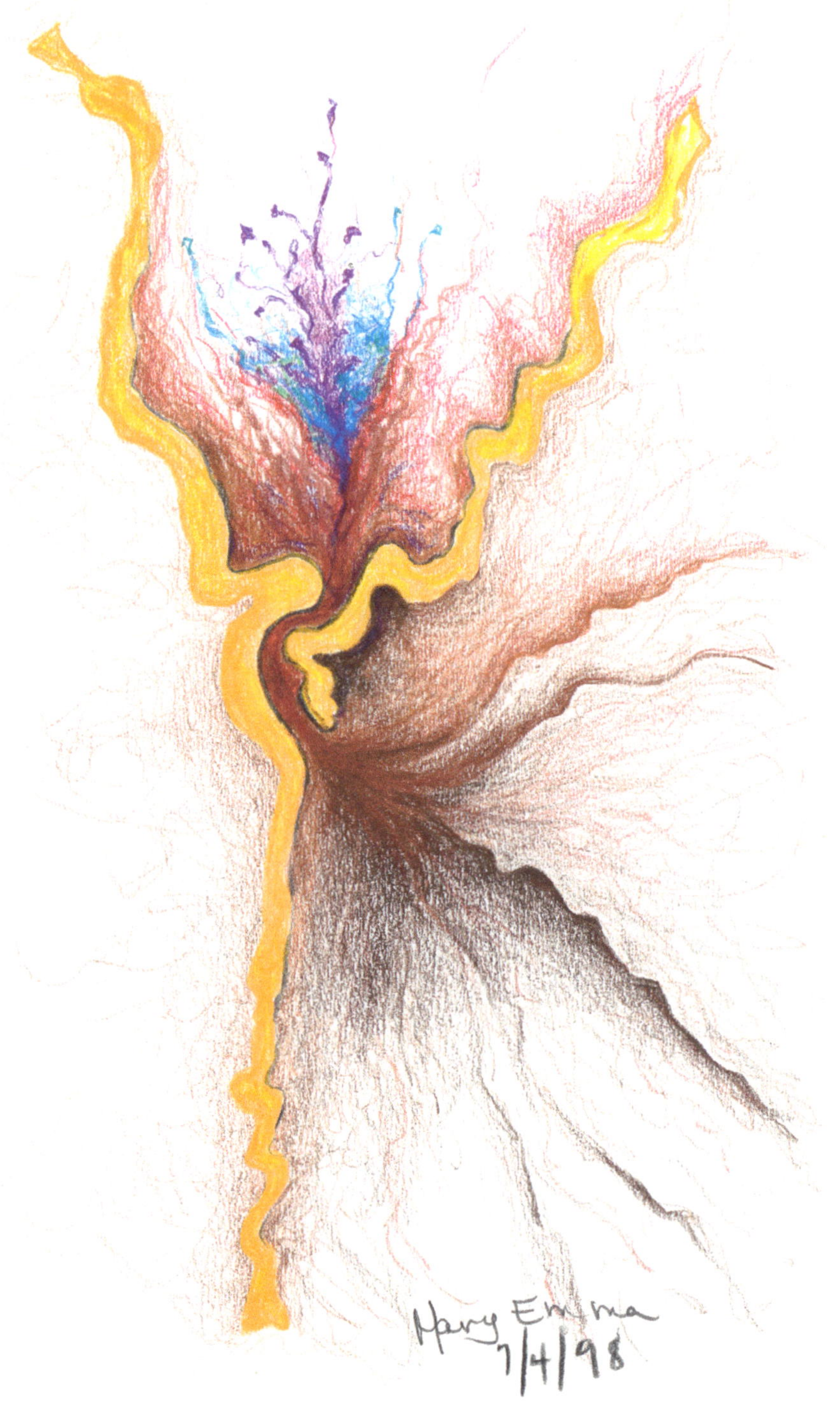

Soft summer rain,
Showering down on flowers, trees, and grass,
    leaving liquid diamond drops to sparkle
    momentarily on the tiny dark green leaves
    of our boxwood bush.
Bathing the parched and dusty earth.

A welcome relief on this steamy summer day.

July 4, 1998

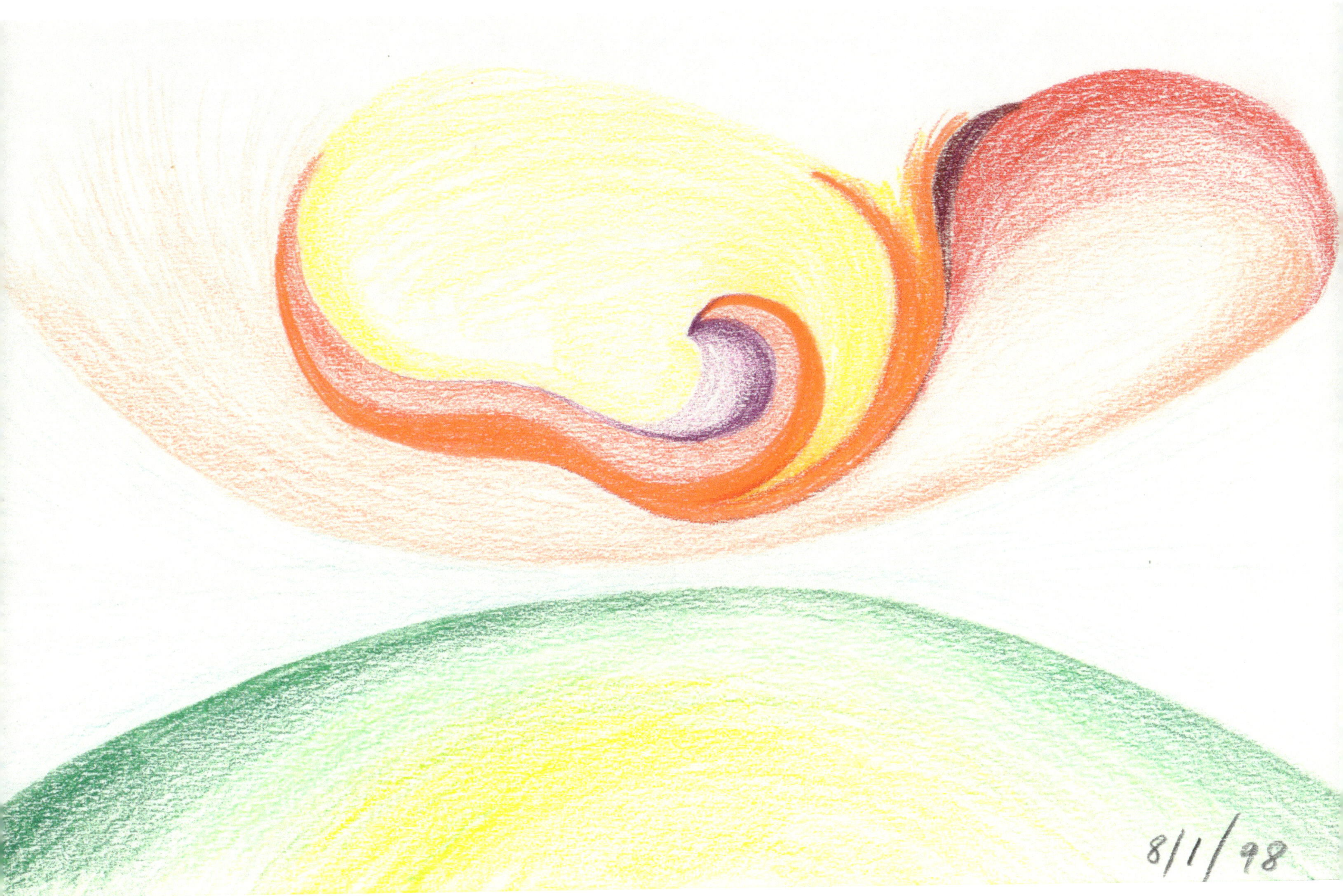
8/1/98

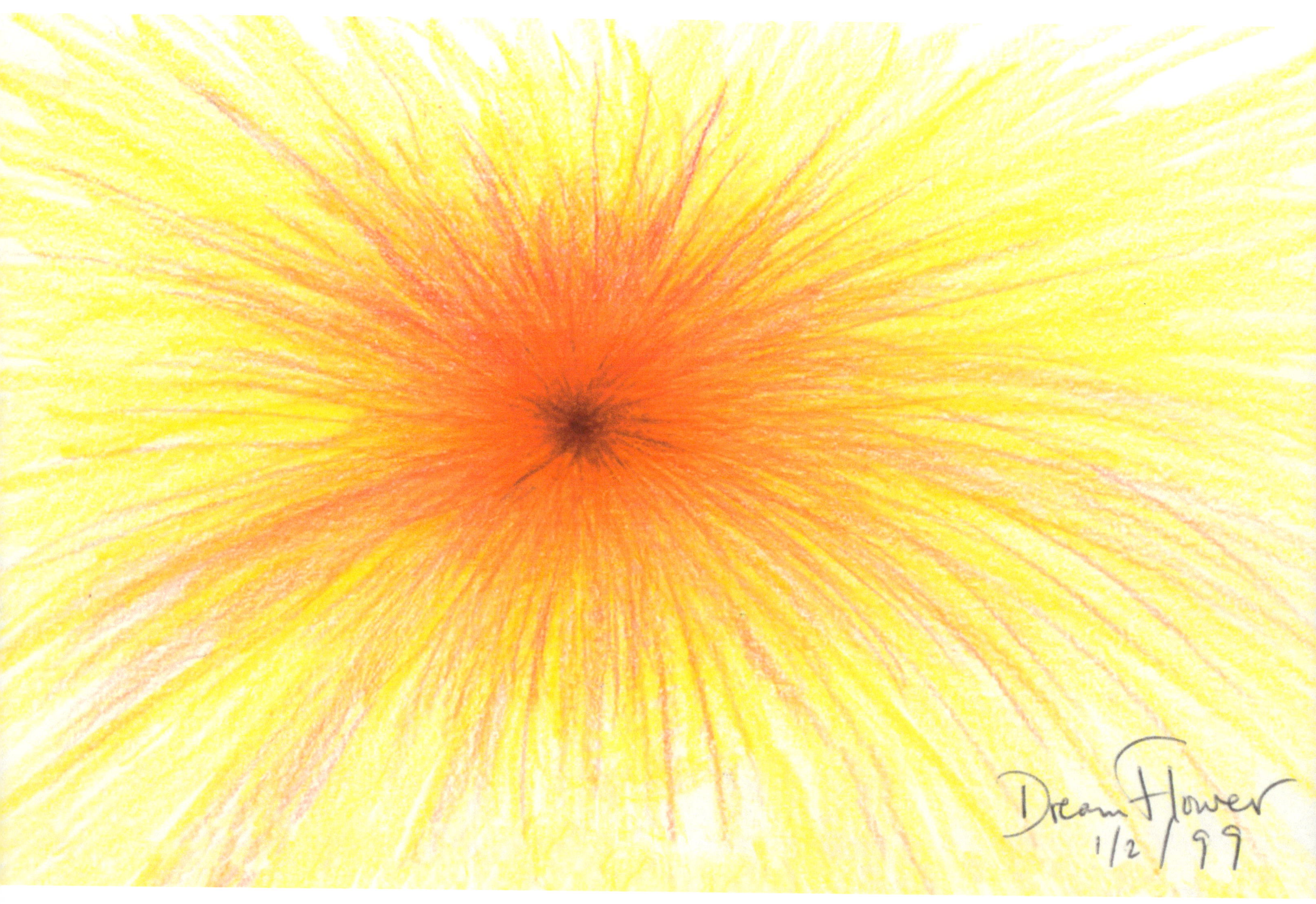
Dream Flower
1/2/99

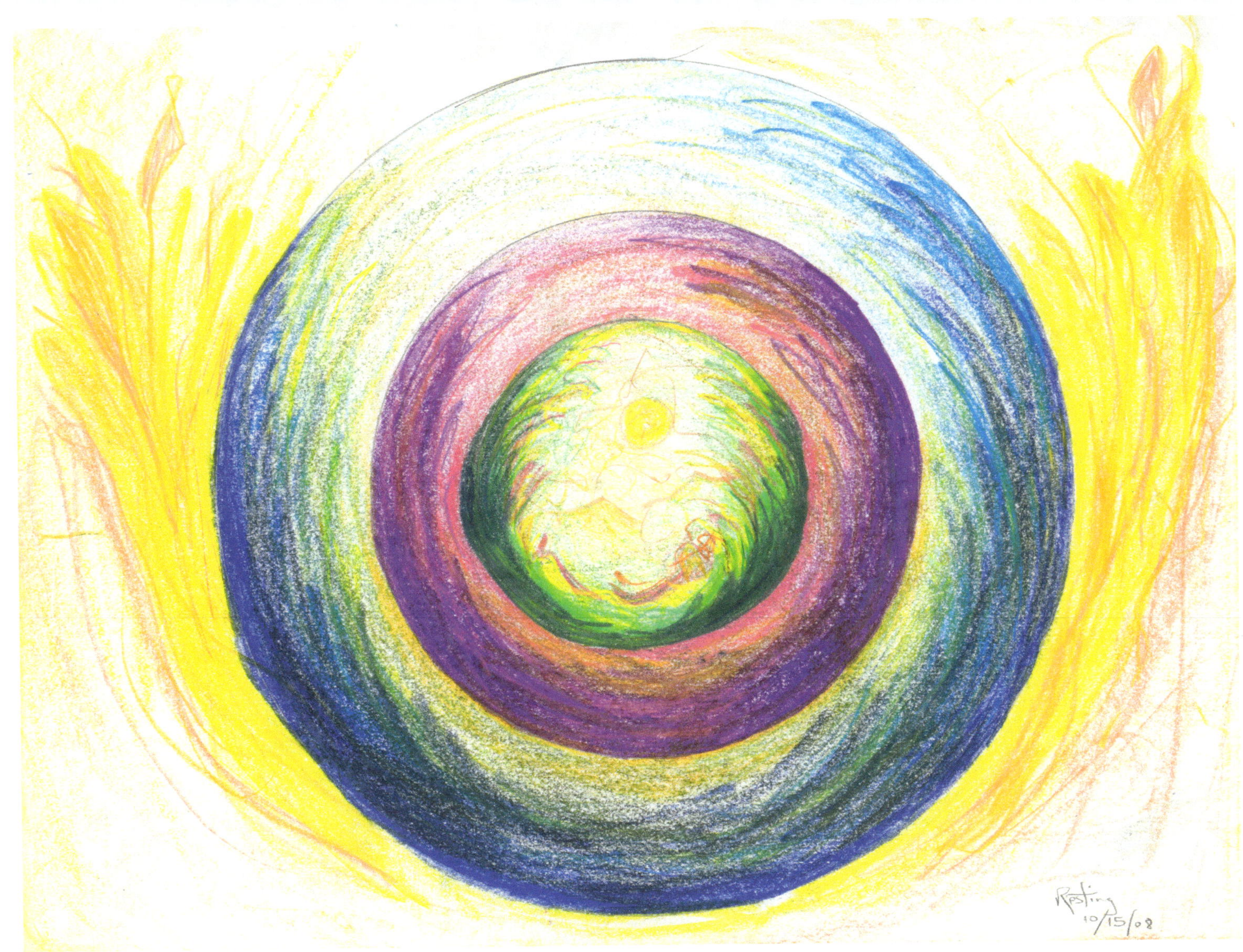

Circles
    Entire worlds
        Holding
            Resting
             Resting
               Resting

October 15, 2008

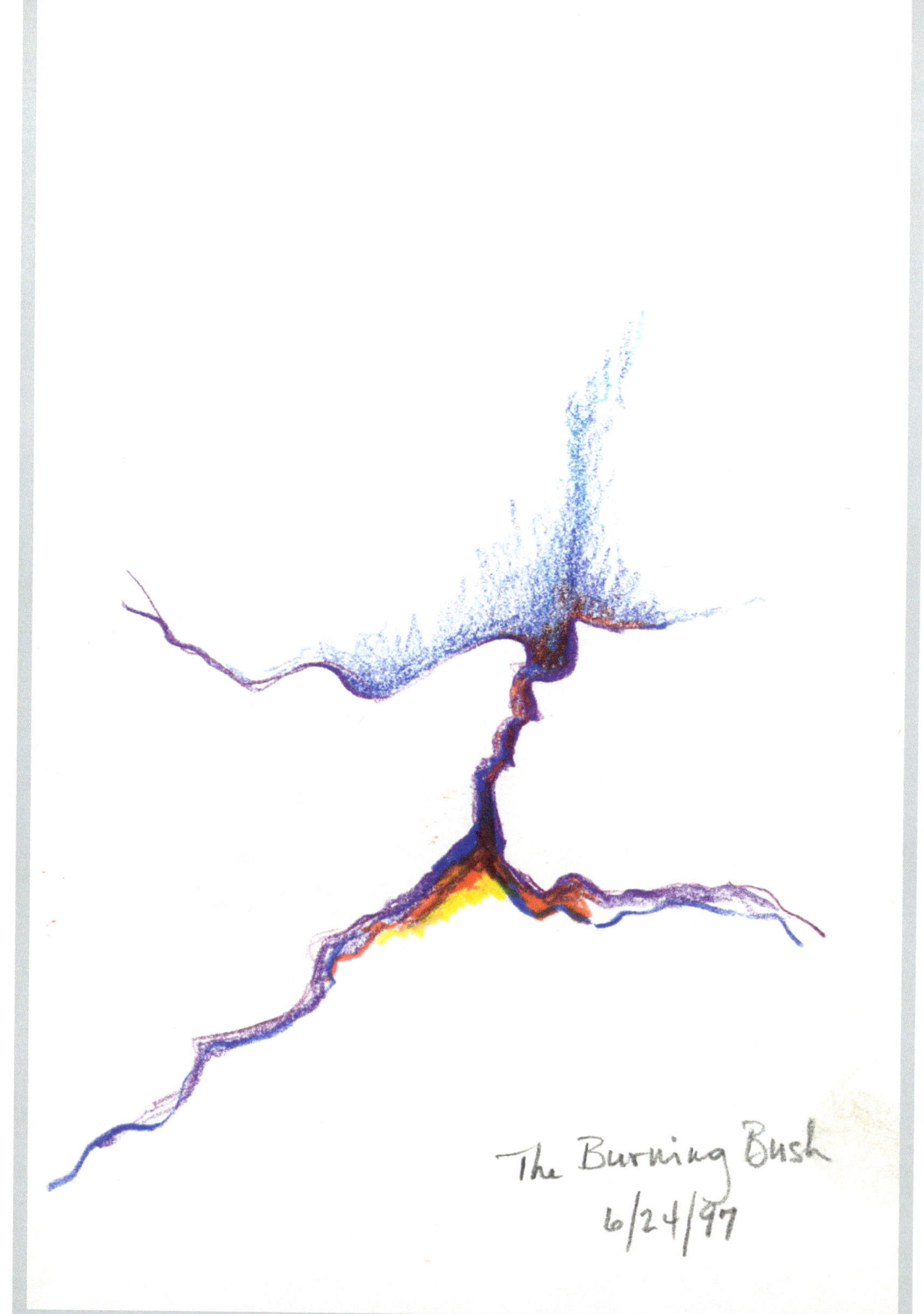
The Burning Bush
6/24/97

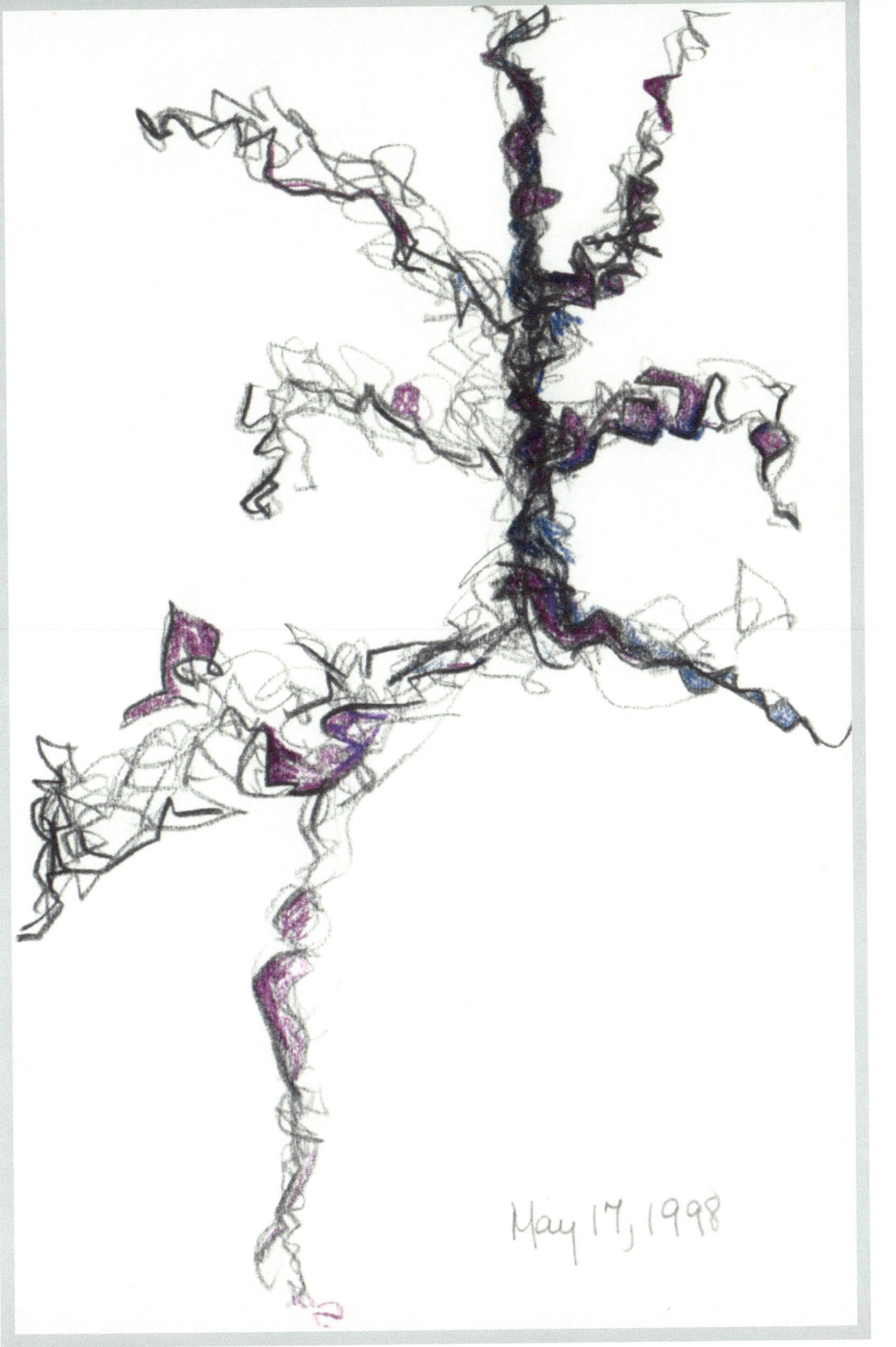

Trust!
Why should I
trust you with
passion and my
tears? Can you
join me in this
space I'm in and
do you know the
dance? Can you breathe
the air I'm breathing?
Can you take the
Chance?

5/17/98

How are you?
    I came home to myself.

How was your trip?
    I went looking for a vision and I found myself.

We're going for breakfast.
    I found a way to feed myself…
    A way to honor my energy
        and my way of knowing

Gotta go…bye…..

May 17, 1998

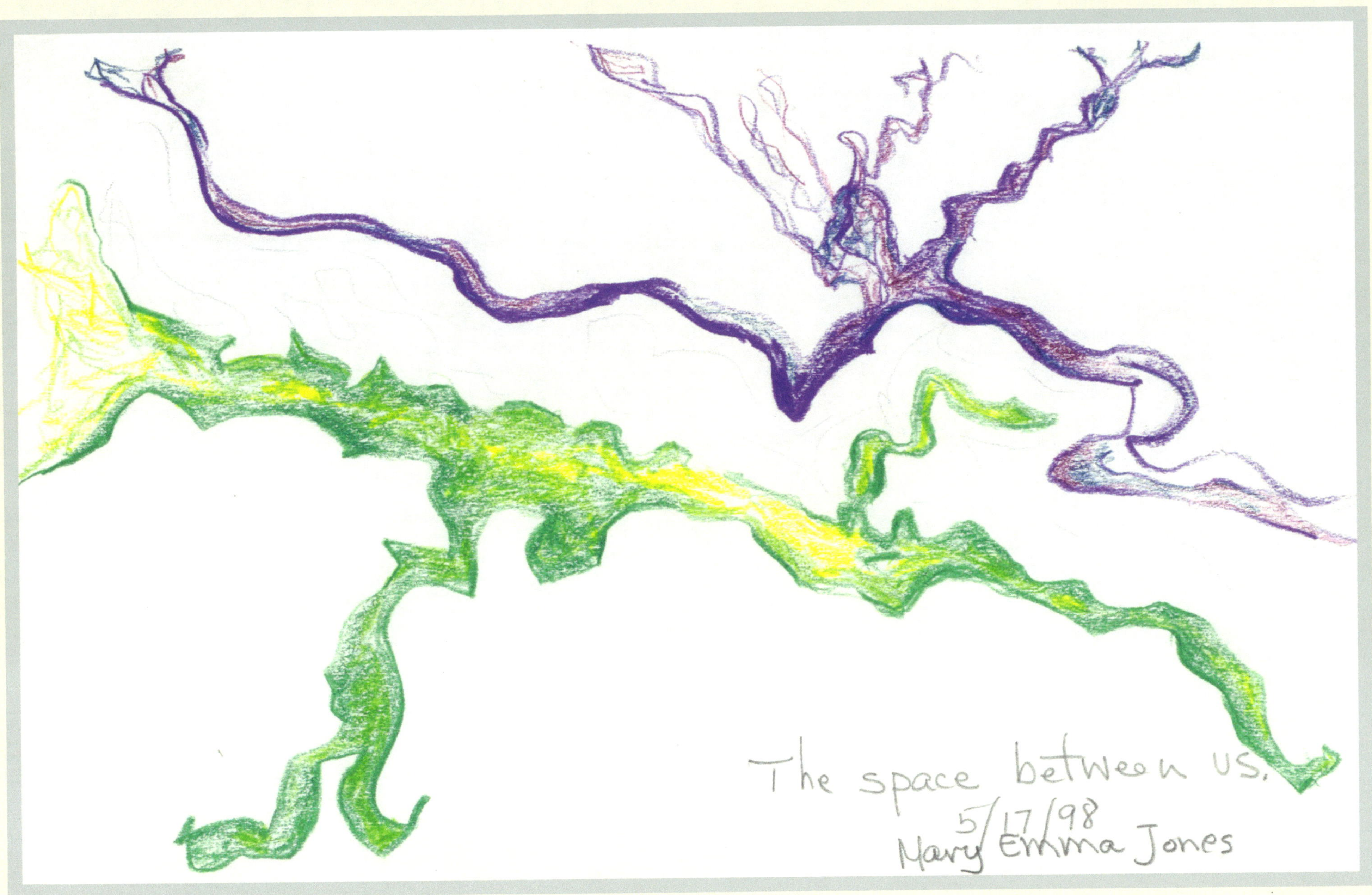
The space between us.
5/17/98
Mary Emma Jones

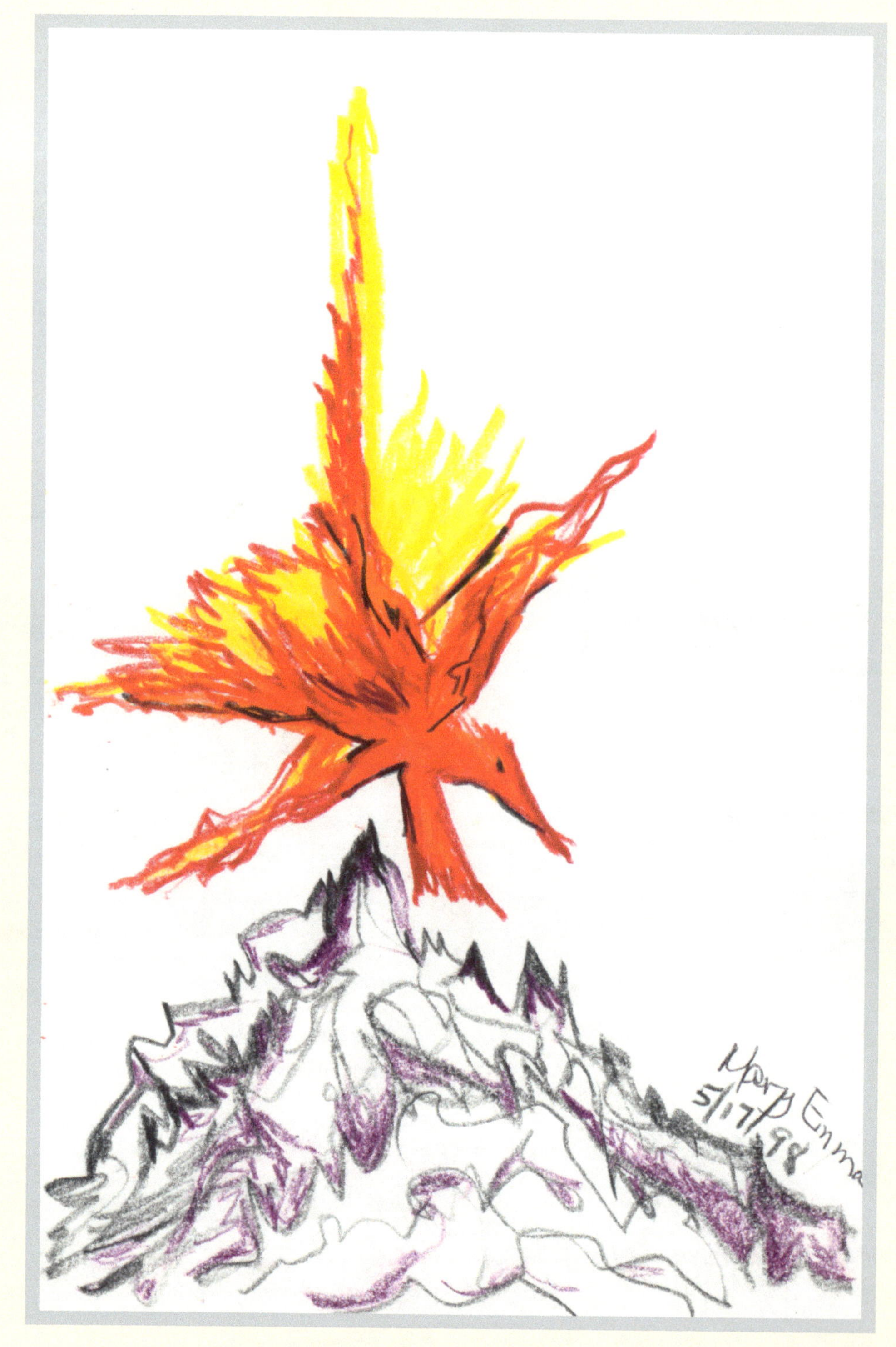

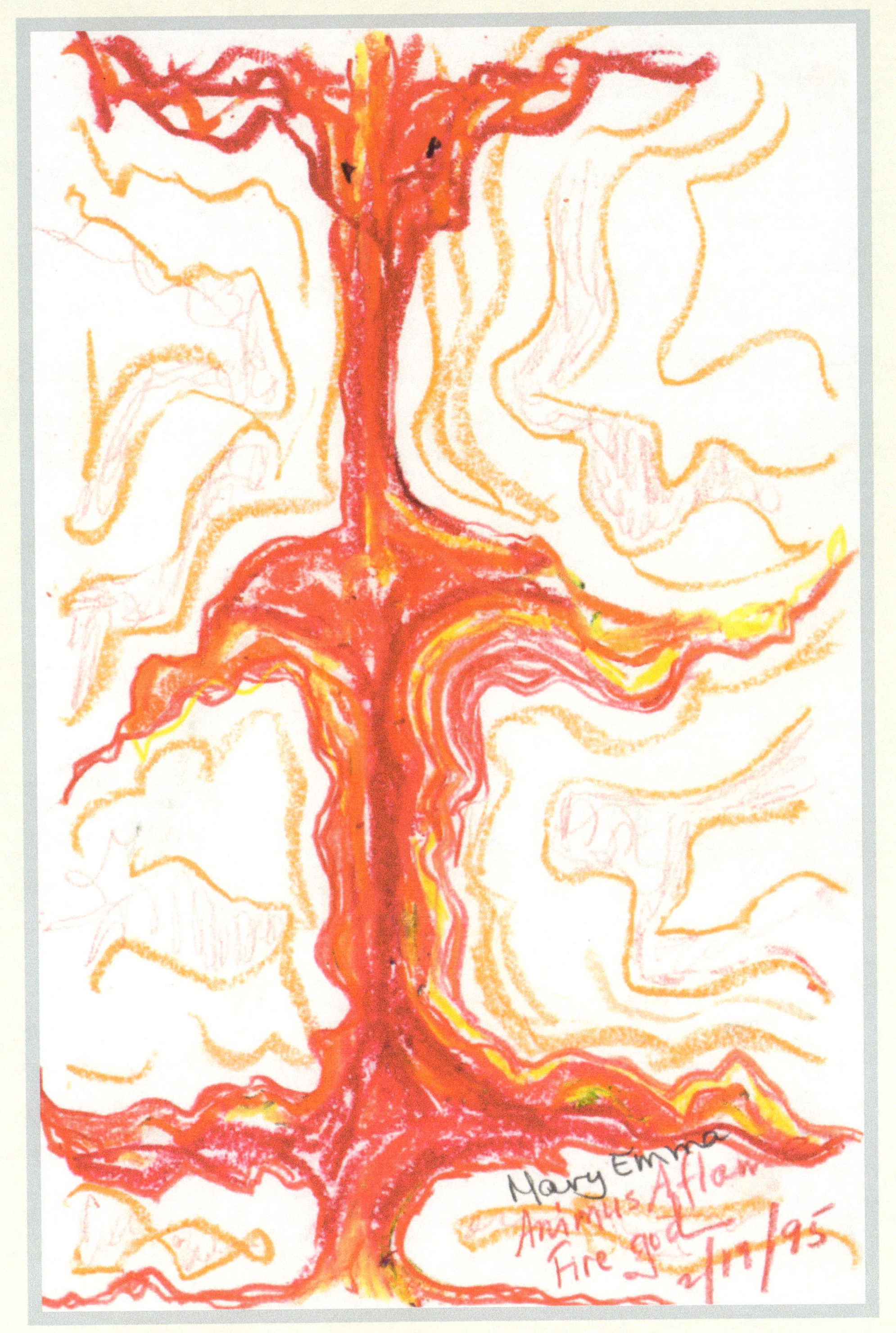

Mary Emma
Animus Aflam
Fire god
2/11/95

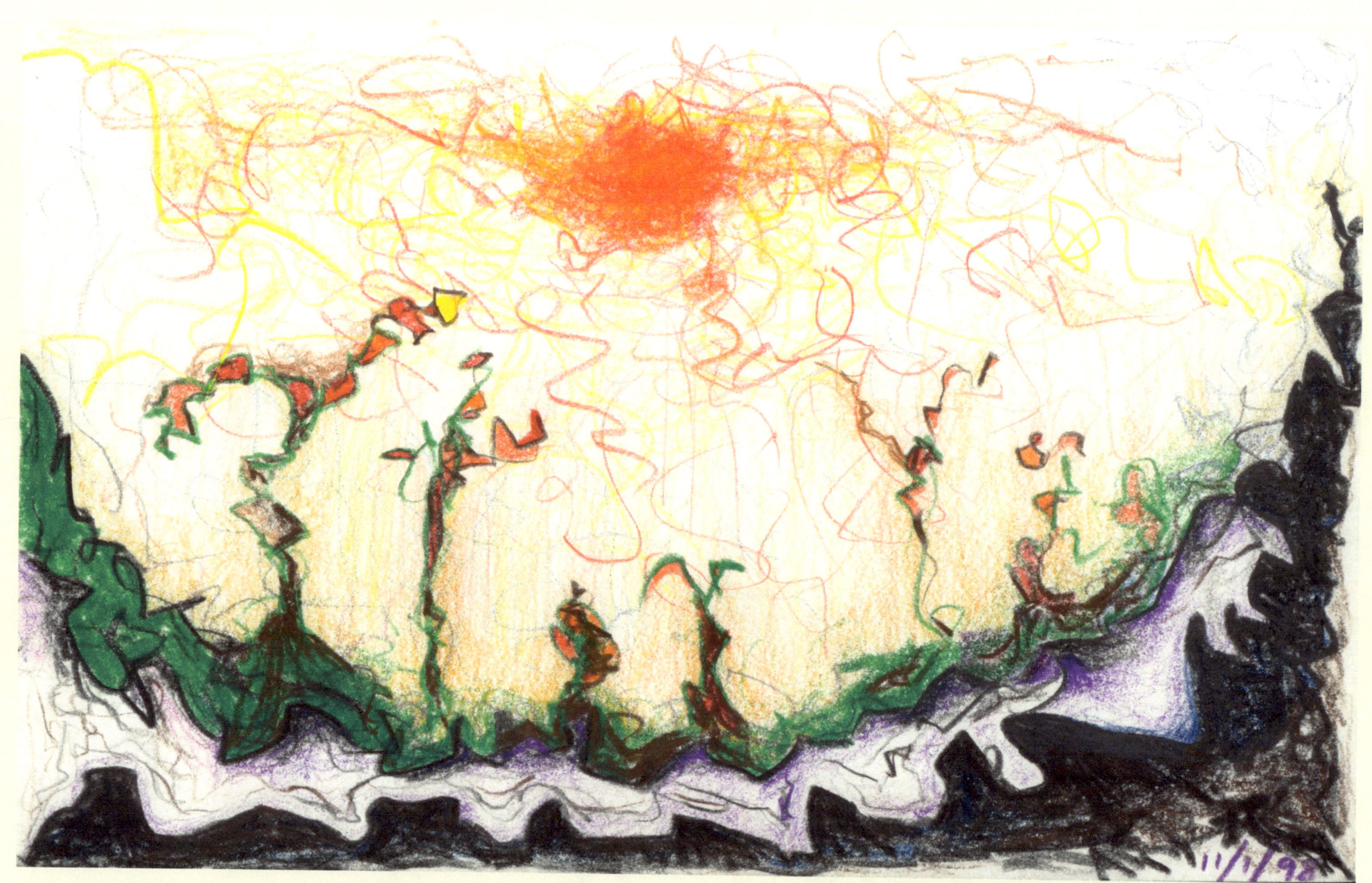

11/17/98

I thought of you today
for the first time in eons…

On Father's Day I missed you.
I felt a sadness that brought tears to my
eyes.

I felt an emptiness that brought pain to
my heart.

I felt your presence in my daughter and
heard your laugh and saw your eyes and
felt your Love.

June 20, 1999

Father Sun
Mother Earth
We praise you

Fill our space
With your warmth

The darkness and the light
Come together in you
And make us whole

Holy is the Spirit of this day

You came to us
Please stay.

November 1, 1998

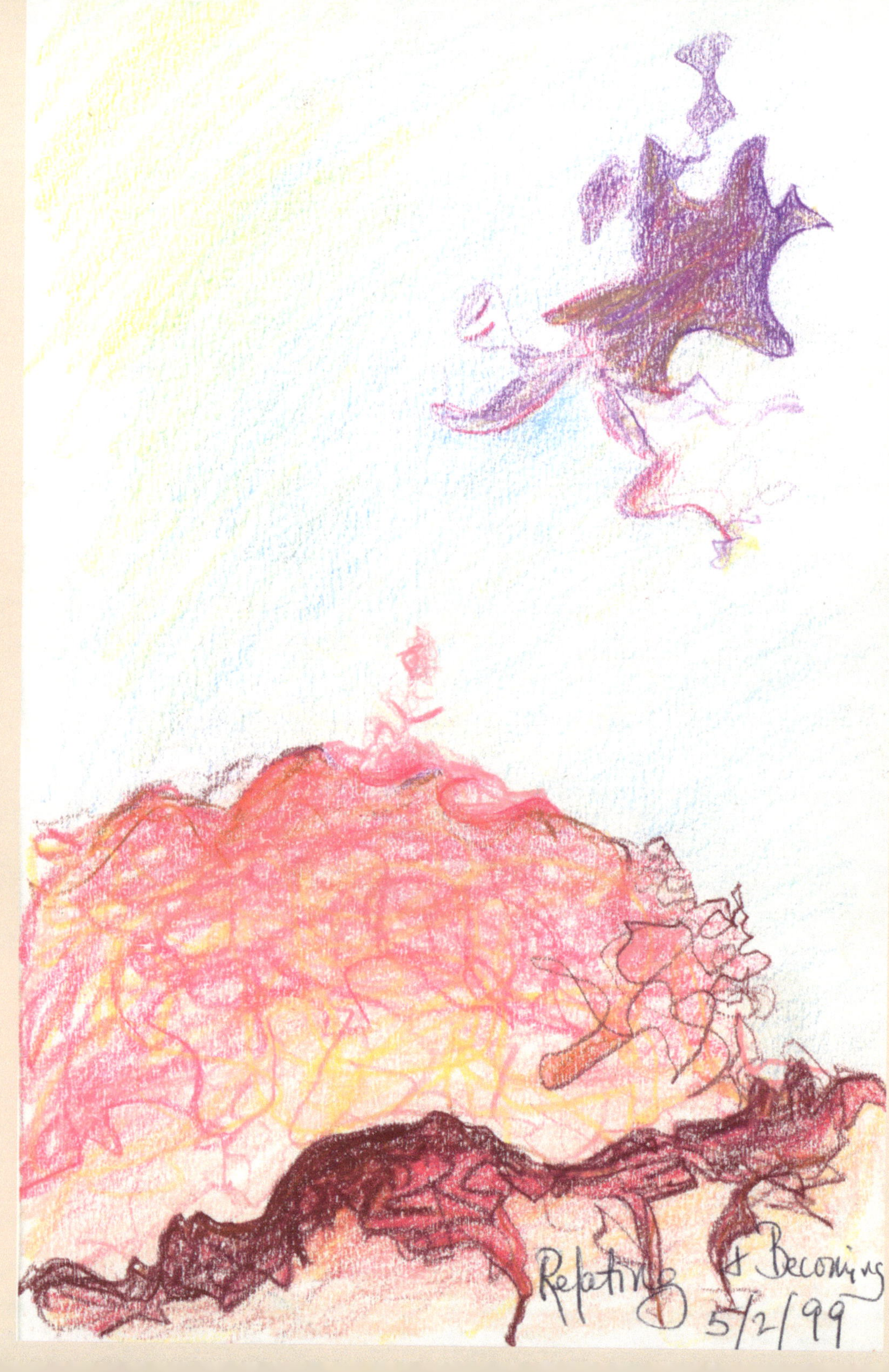

Delicate threads of light
Form spider home
Held aloft by last year's cattail at
The edge of the pond.

Shimmering reflections
Of dogwood blossoms
Silently announce it is spring.

May 2, 1999

I feel the strength of your spirit
Supporting and caressing
My true voice,
which comes from deep inside my
being.

November 29, 1998

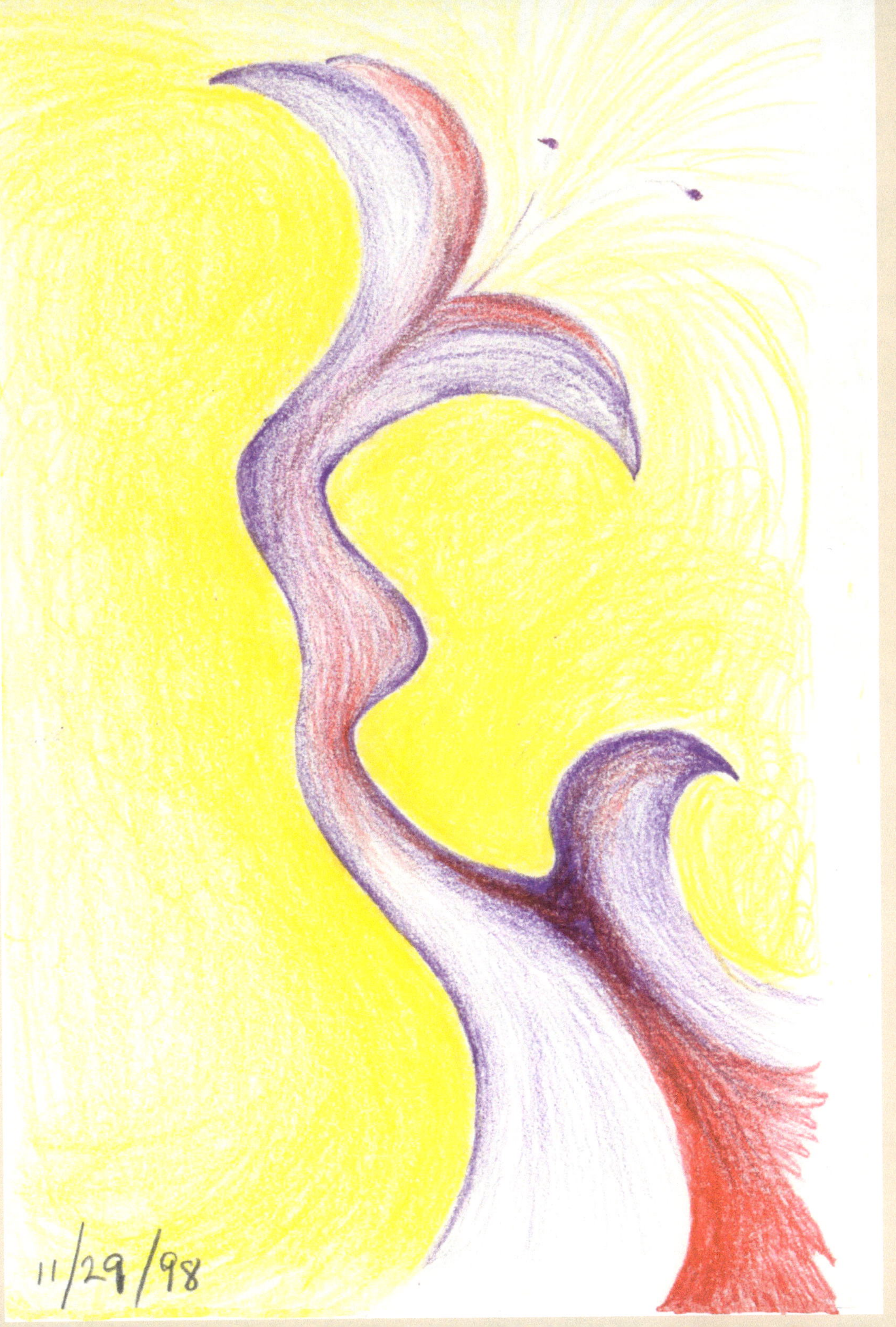

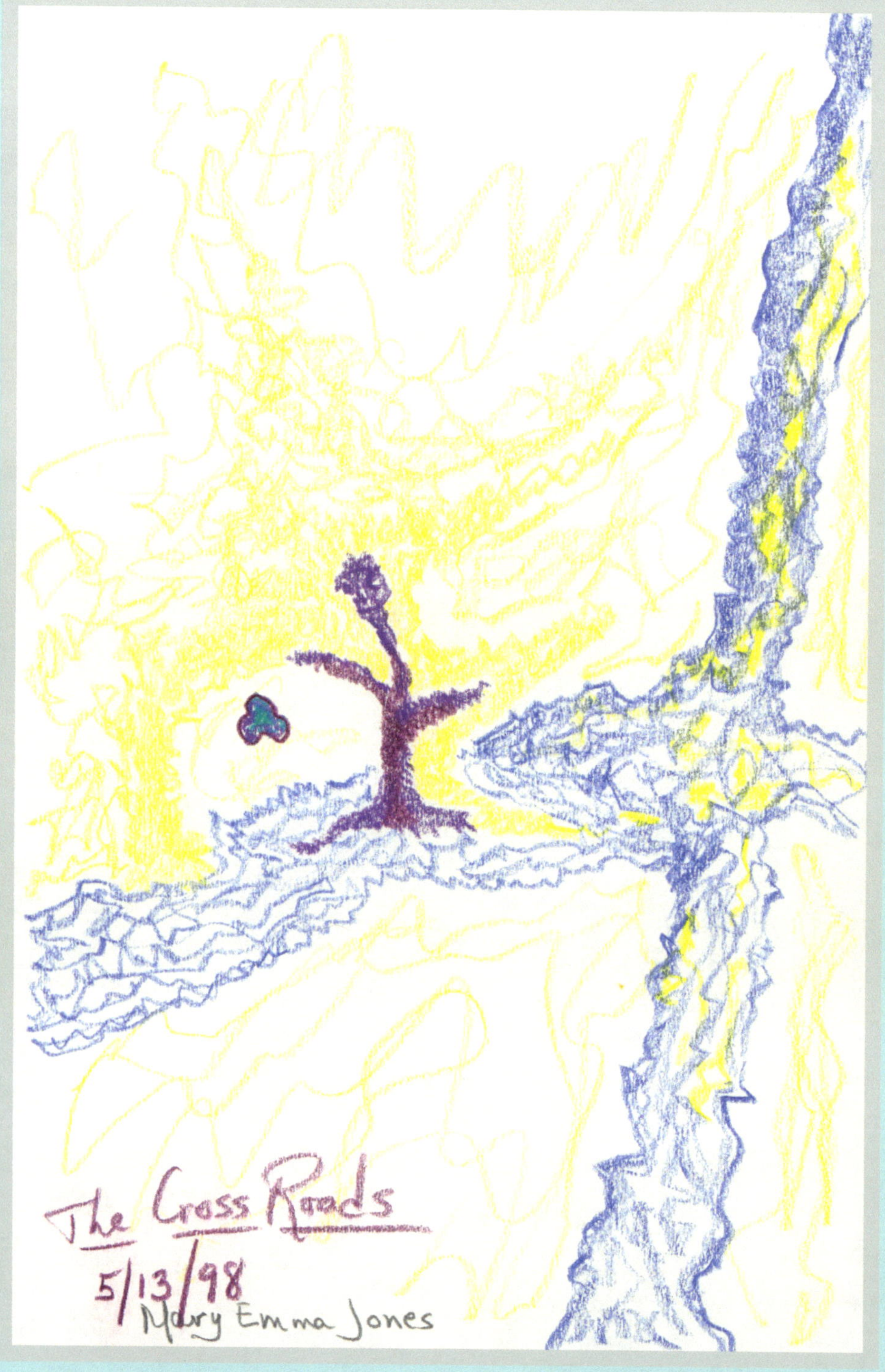

On a Journey into Wholeness conference on St. Simon's Island in 1998, I drove over to the beach and wrote:

Sitting on this sheltered corner of a quiet beach, an embankment of wet gray rocks on one side and remnants of an ancient pier on the other,
I remember the spot nearby where, on a summer day so many years ago our young family sat in the sand making a sand castle...Dripping wet sand into delicate towers for fantasy and fun.

As the wet sand dribbled through my fingers, I came alive inside myself. My daughter laughed with joy. My baby son lay peacefully in his carrier. All the while my husband looked quietly on.

May 13, 1998

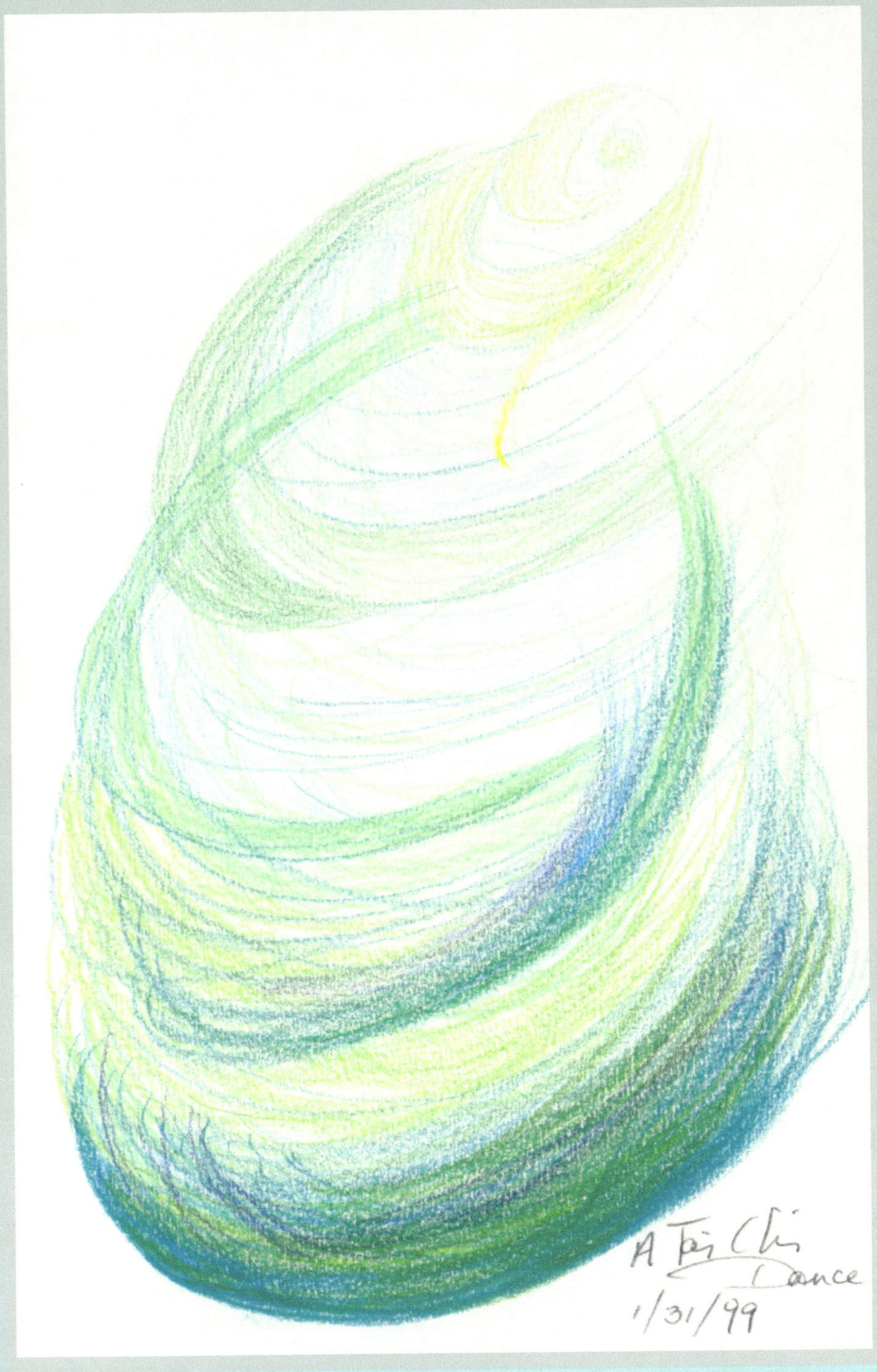

I only thought you were lost.
You were there all the time…
     Waiting
          Waiting
For color and shape to define you
For tenderness to release you
For love to welcome you home.

So sing now that I might hear you
Give me shape and color and tell me my name.

In the summer of 2003 in the time of Amma's
birthday, she gave me my name. Sumati.

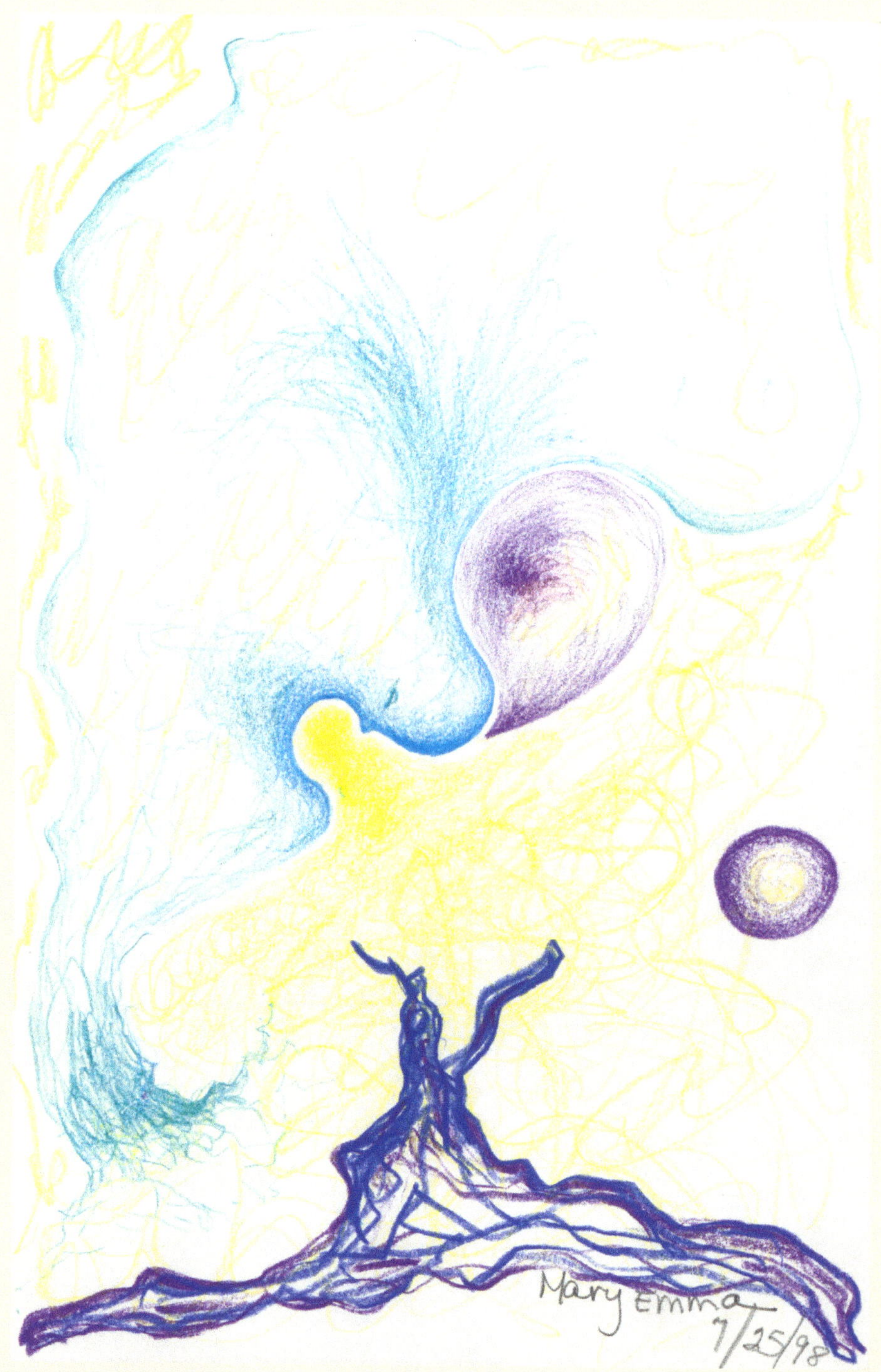

Please come.

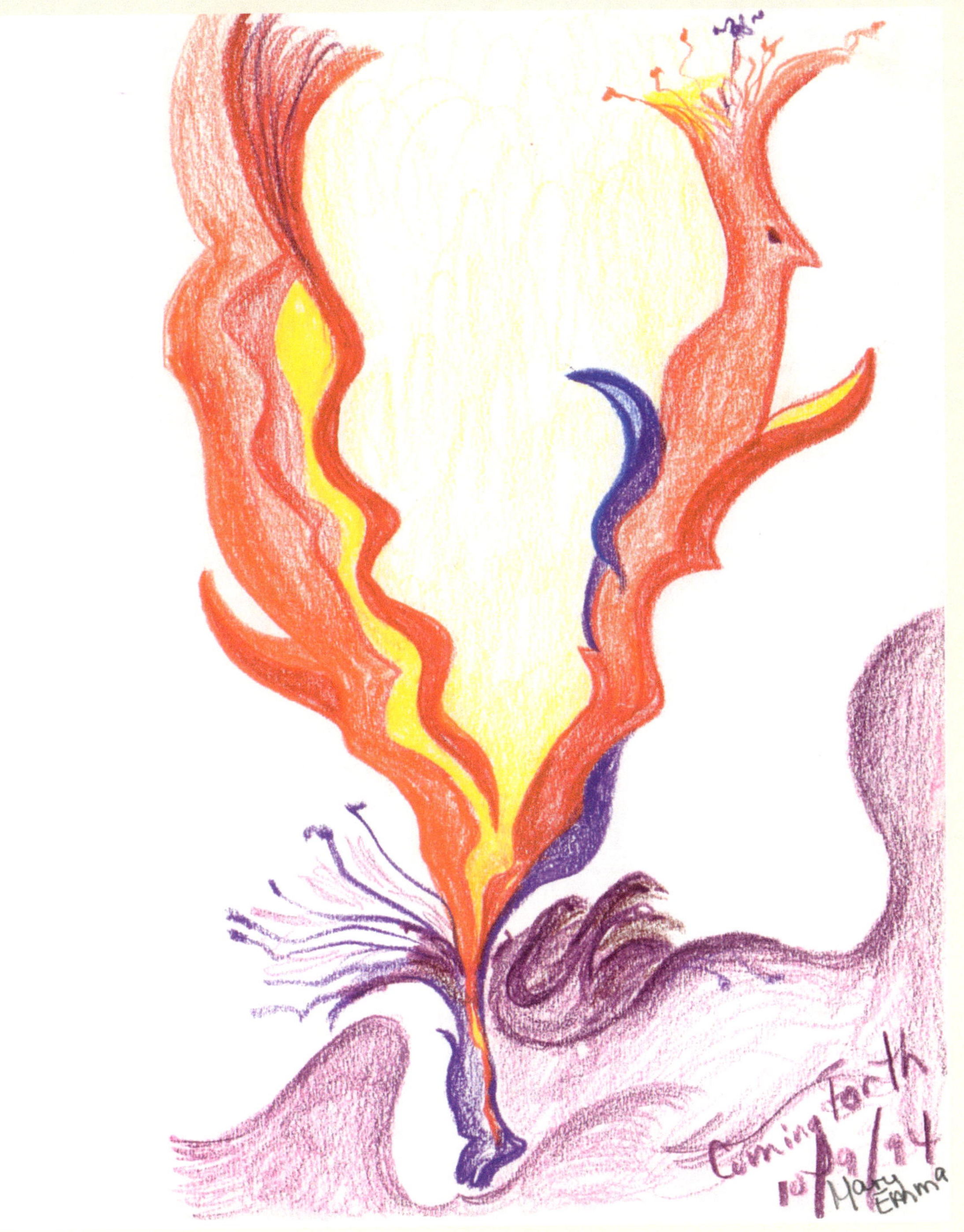

Coming forth.

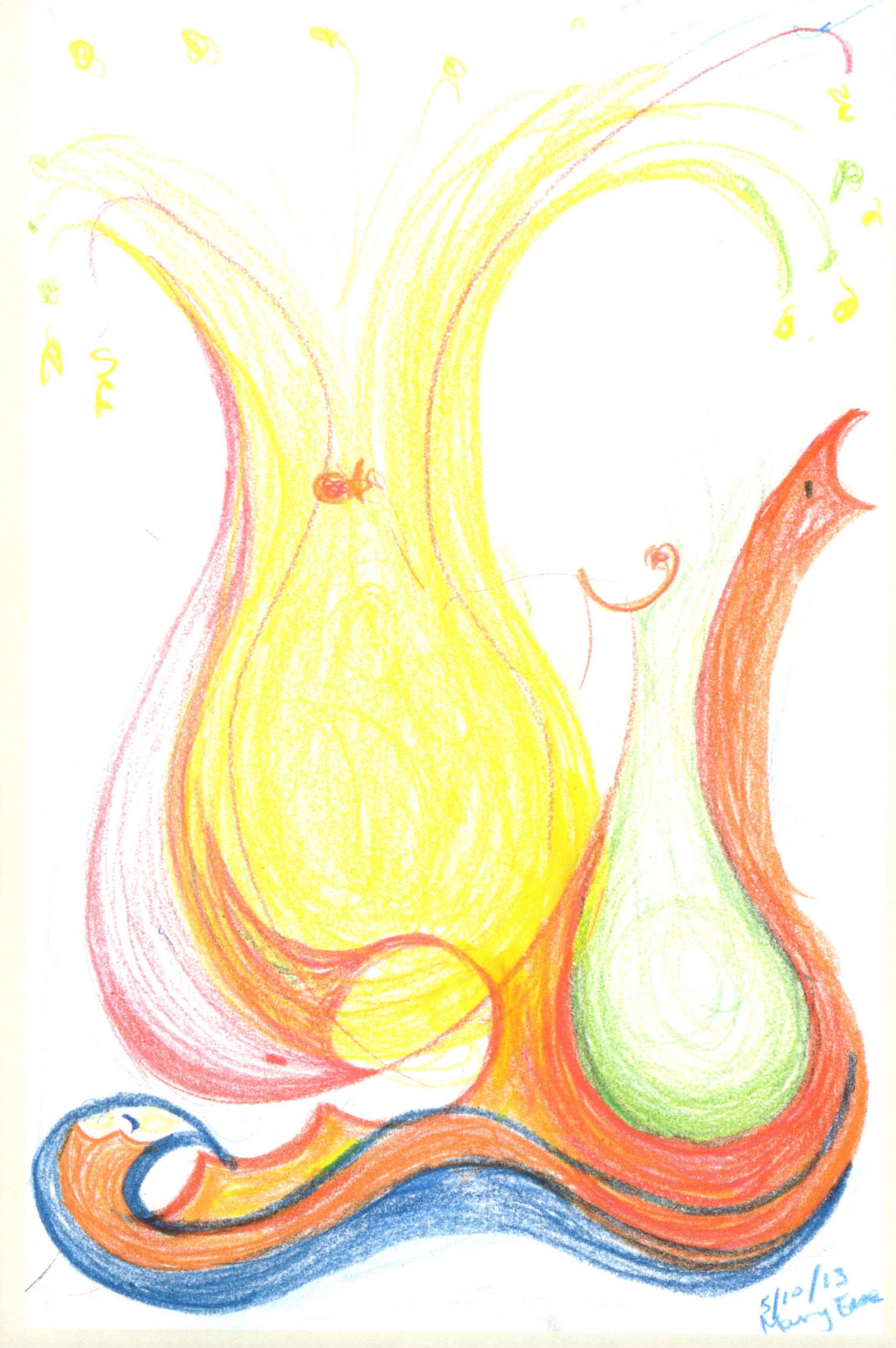

Sacred fire
   Sacred vessels
      Sleeping birds
         Waiting for the Awakening

———————

Awaken now
  The time has come
     The fire is contained
       The vessels are full
          for NOW

The time is NOW
     Come beloved
     Dance with me
     Drum for me
     Sing for me

I am listening to your song.

May 10, 2013

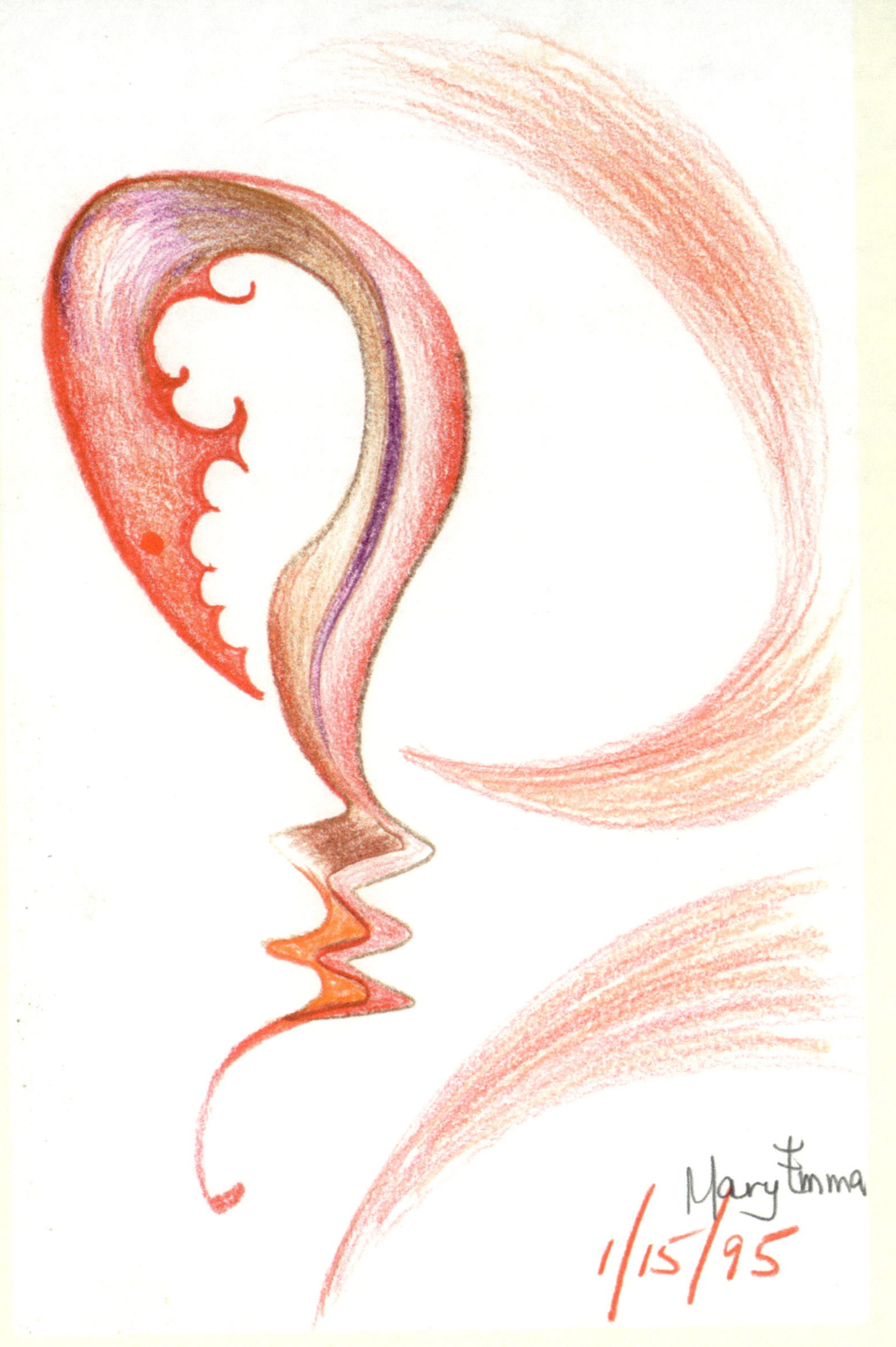
Mary Emma
1/15/95

On some distant butte we met
We knew each other so well
And yet…
We were strangers
From far distant places
Come together to
Share our lives
Perhaps to teach each other
A wisdom
Yet unknown
Surely to love each other
In a new unfamiliar way
Across time and space I feel
Your presence

Come…
Let us celebrate
Let us sing and dance
Among the stars
That are our home.

July 25, 1999

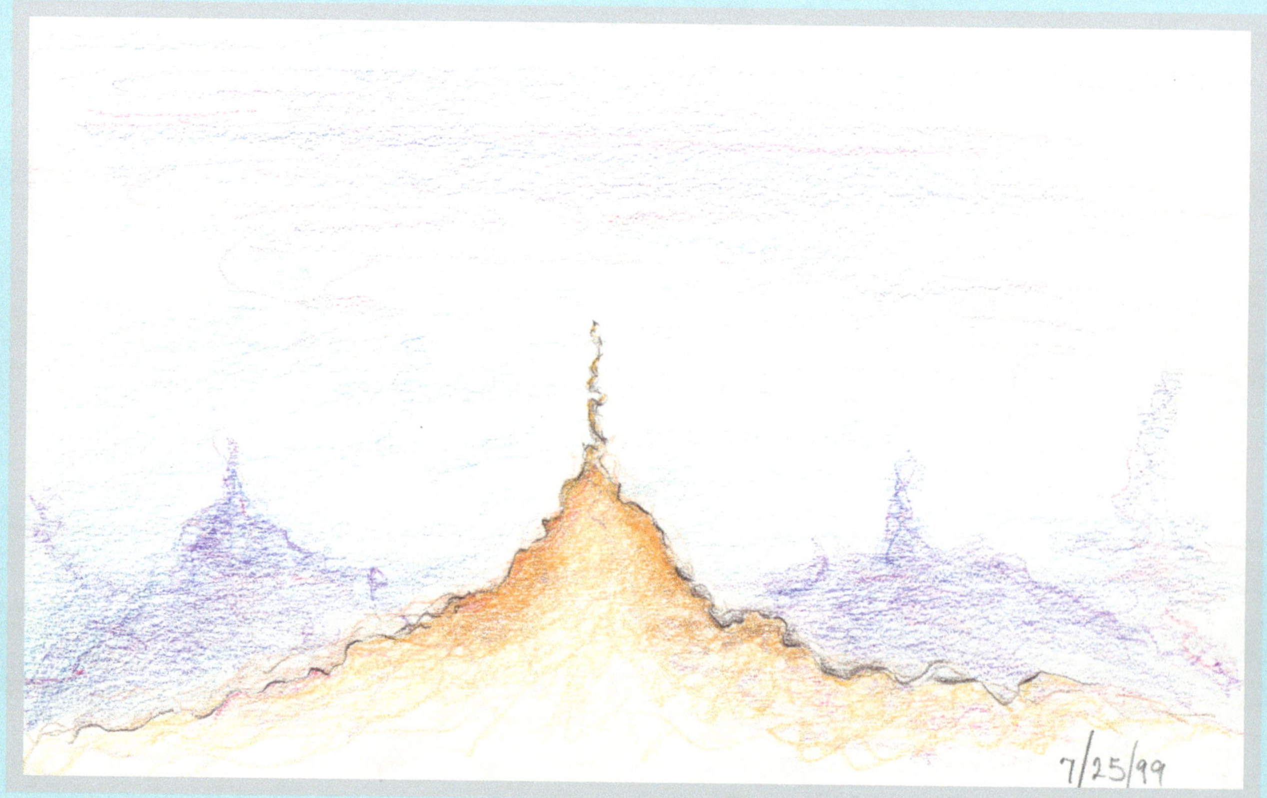

How can I contain myself
    When the coming feels so strong?
How can I contain myself
    When the coming has been so long?

The energy from the depths
    Pushes upward toward the sky
    Held for now by the thinnest film
I can see through it.
    I can move through it.
        I can fly!

The film can stretch
    With the power of the sea
While the disparate parts of myself unite
    Longing to be free.

November 30, 2015

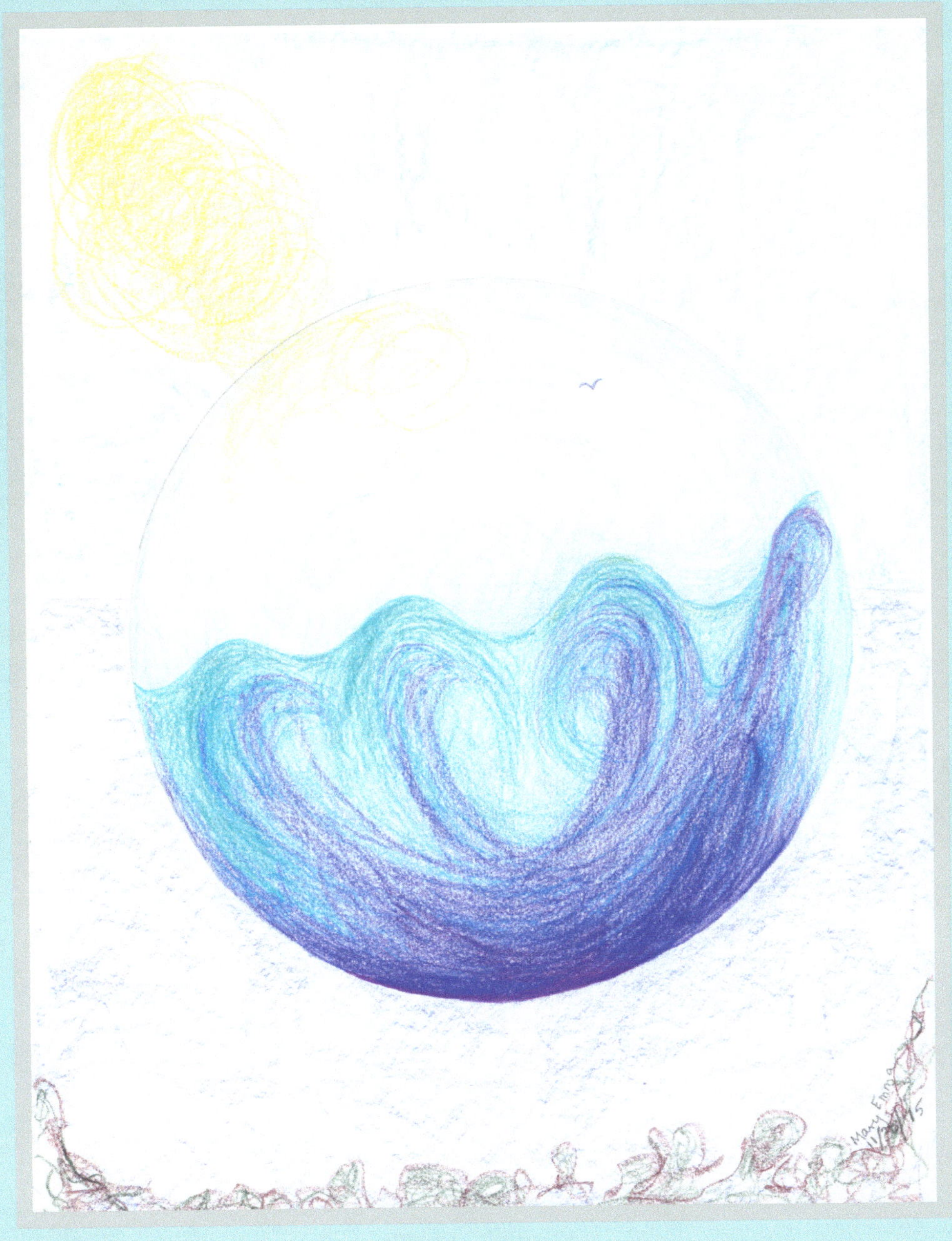

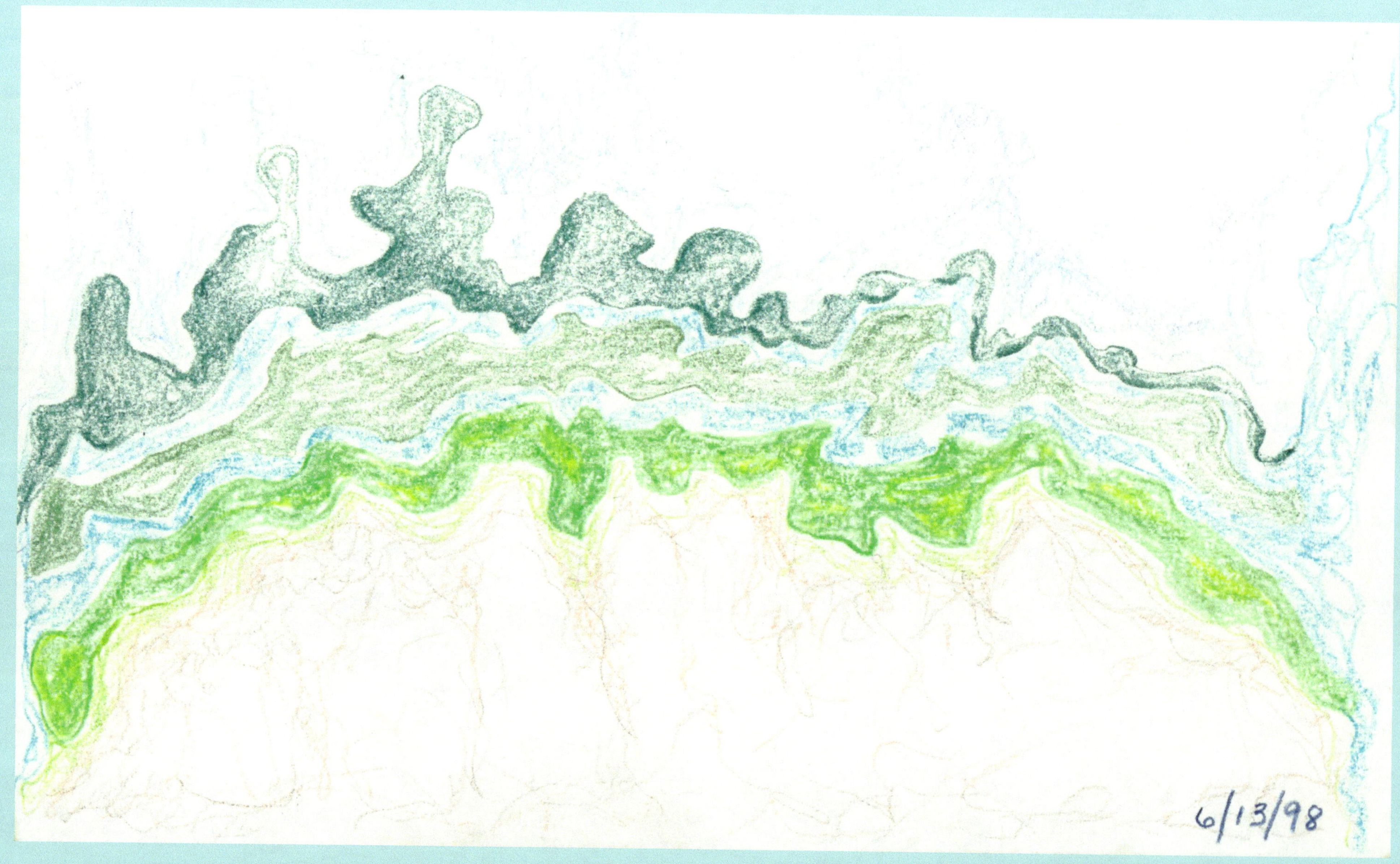

6/13/98

Softly the day surrounds me.
Gently the mountains hold me.
The pond supports me.
And I feel peace.

June 13, 1998

Nurturing myself in this cocoon of a
cove
Sky above; pond below…
I wait…
I rest…
I know…

June 13, 1998

Dream,
You're a slide that's out of focus in a projector
that does not always work.
You've collected dust on some hidden shelf
And now I am ready for you, but I am not sure
where you are!

So I will wait and rest and hope…
I will look for any glimmer…
And I will try to trust that the process of
dreaming has a life of its own.

April 12, 1998

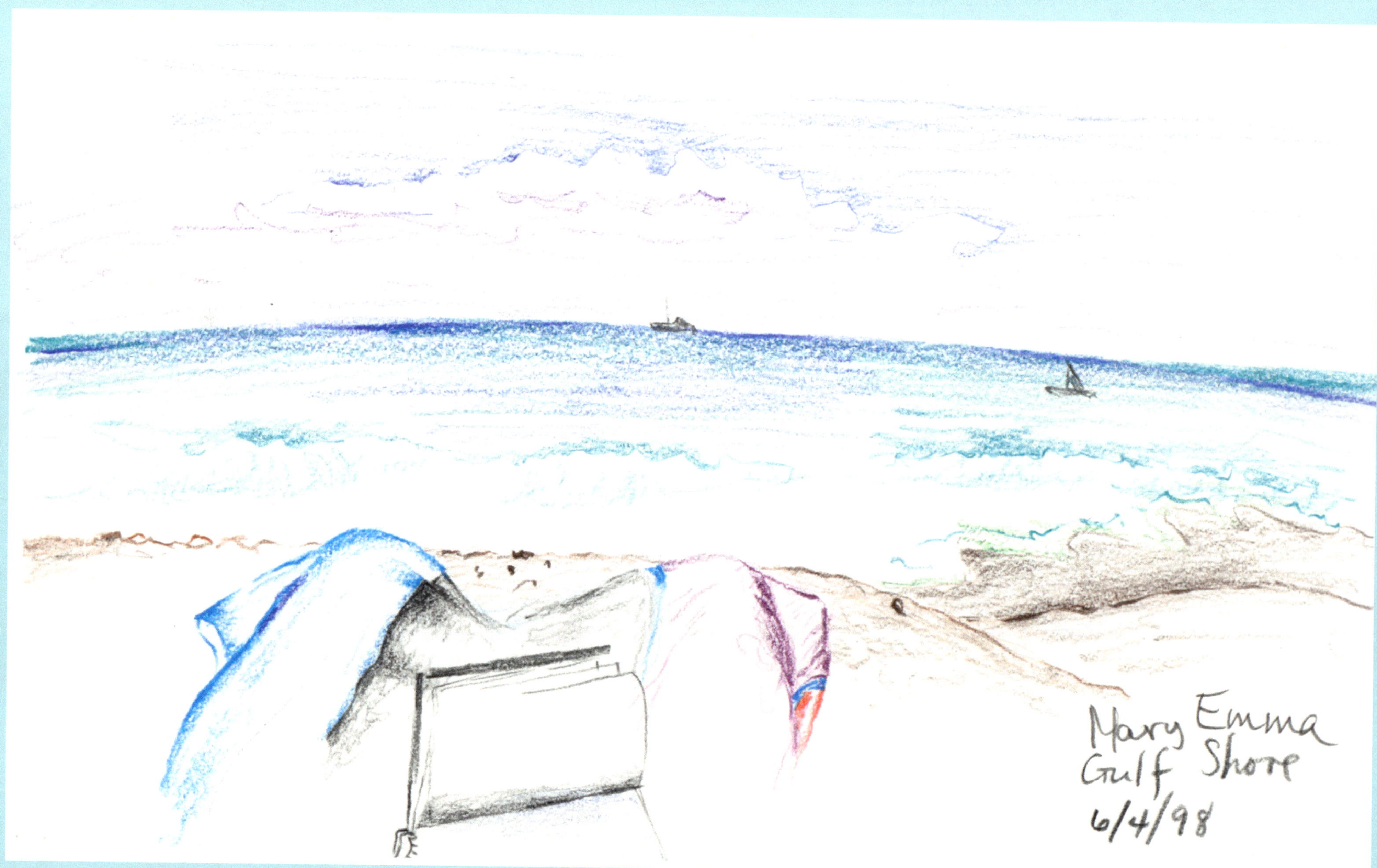
Mary Emma
Gulf Shore
6/4/98

Mother Ocean
She touched my feet and
I sang…
She washed over me and danced around me
Touching the sky
Caressing the earth
Sparkling
Throbbing
Inviting us to
Play

August 21, 1999

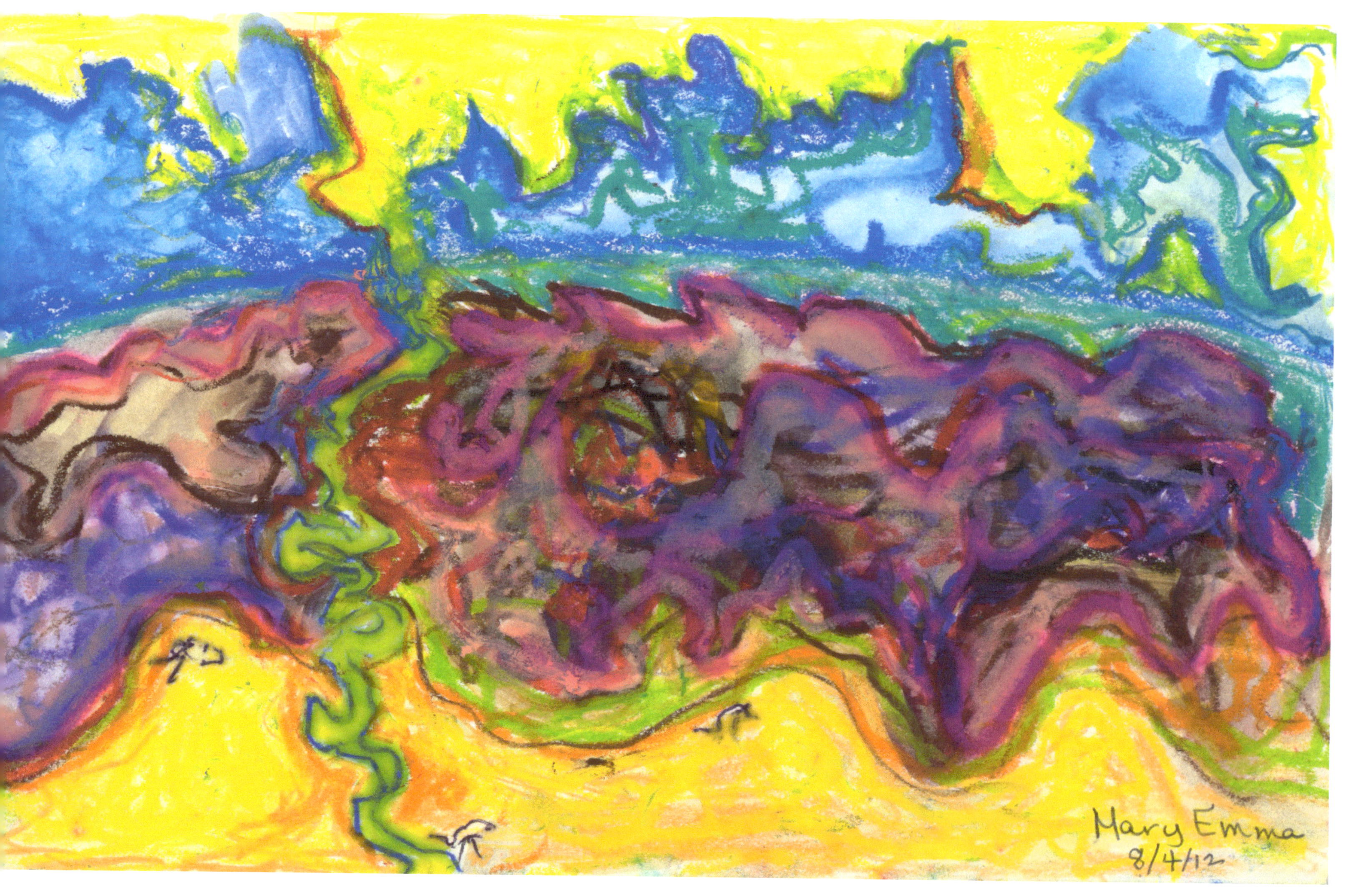
Mary Emma
8/4/12

Waiting for the words,
        I watch the waves of the Atlantic
            Caress the shore.
Sandpipers scurry along its edge
        Artfully dodging the approaching foam.

Kuş, küçük kuş
    Sana bakıyorum.
        Deniz geliyor. Deniz gidiyor.
            Yemek yiyorsunuz.
                Içiyorsunuz, sizi dinledim.

Bird, Small Bird
    I am watching you.
        The sea is coming. The sea is going.
            You are eating your dinner.
                You drank, bird; I listened.

August 4, 2012

A friendly shape. You appeared amidst the chaos of my mind and watched
    Kindly
      Intently
And ever so carefully as the light came down from above making its way through the winding channel to the sandy earth where hungry sandpiper and long-legged bird searched for tidbits of food along the shifting shoreline
    Kuş Adası

August 4, 2012

The day stretches out in front of me.
No watch. No plan to stop its flow.
Surrounded by bird song and
creek splash,
I rest
and I watch
Gently swaying asters and daisies
Tiny lavender butterflies
Fluttering by
Dragonfly darting in and out of
Sunlight
And the shimmering surface
Of our pond rippling and
Sparkling over its
Reflections of the
Wolf Pen Range in shades of
Brown and green.

June 6, 1998

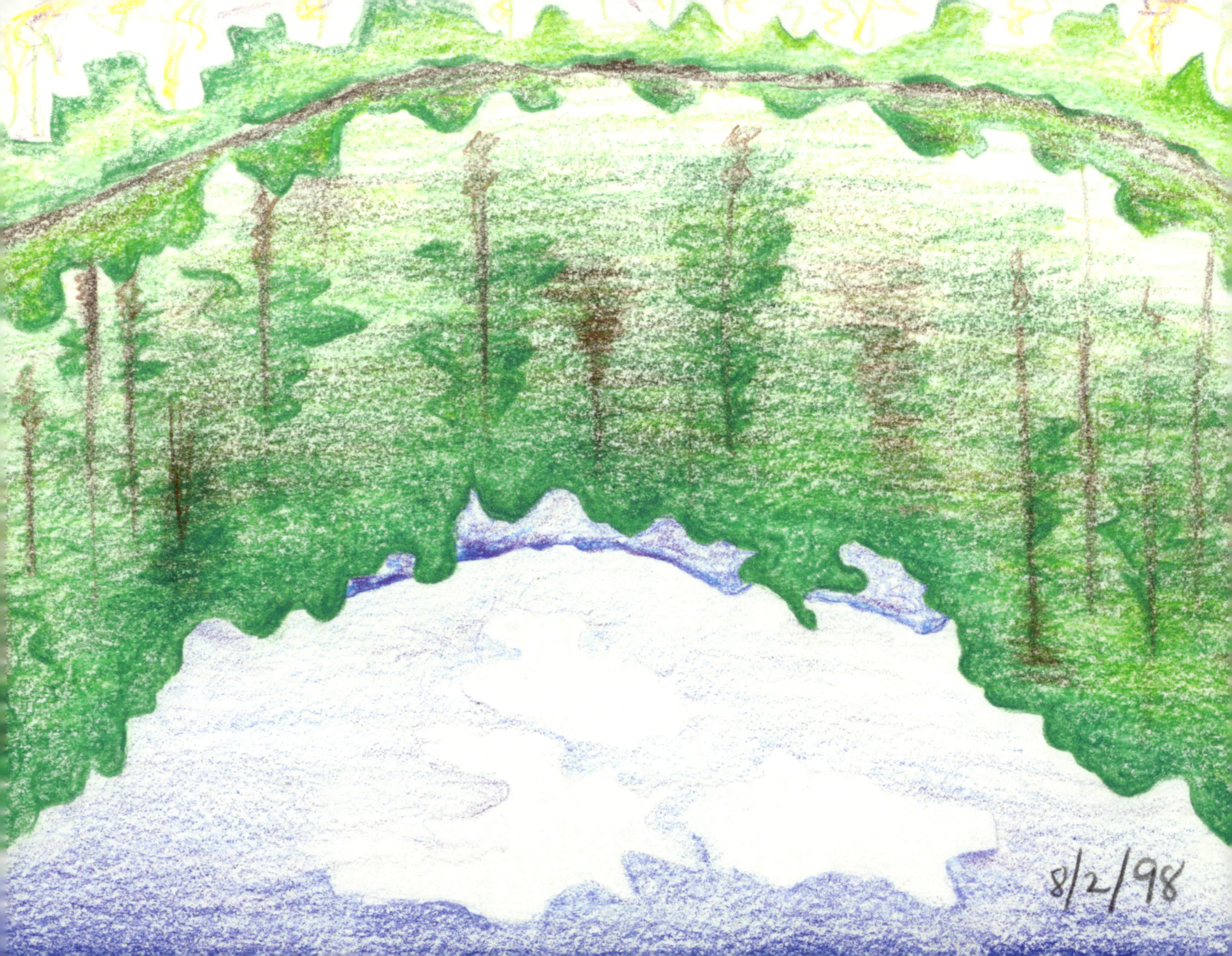

8/2/98

On the back side of summer
Stately Joe Pye weed makes its annual pronouncement
That school is about to begin
Goldenrod in bunches beckon
The student and teacher alike
To return to the classroom.
Tiger swallow tail flits merrily about
ignoring these grave pronouncements
As do I – seated comfortably on the dock of the pond
contemplating my new freedom and smiling.

August 2, 1998

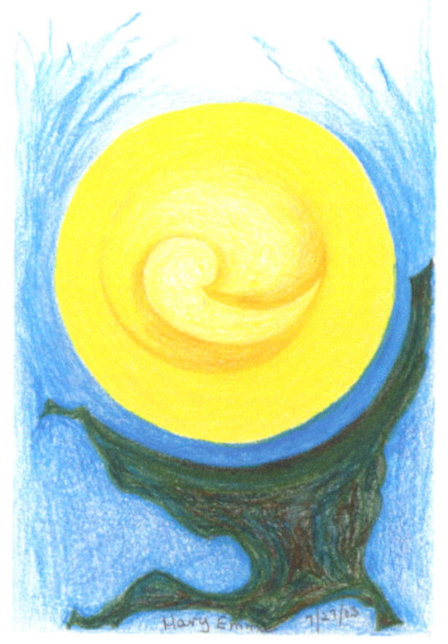

Hold me
As I unfold in your arms
Cradle me
    As I learn my song.
Shelter me
    As my wings grow strong
Release me
    With the faith that you
    are always there
To hold me in your heart.

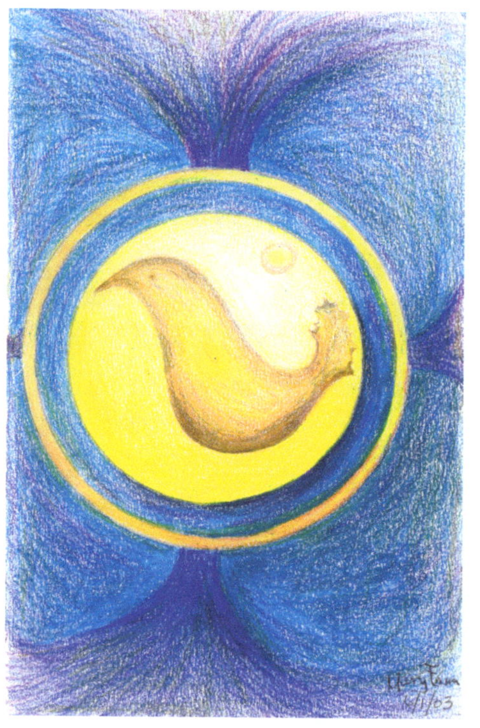

July 27, 2003

Once Again

Once Again
I wait to be born
Into a new day

Once again
I find myself waiting
to be born into
Ecstasy and Wonder

Into a world that
sparkles with love
Into a world where
darkness holds potential
for terror and
for growth

A world that waits
for me to awake
and be born into the
new day

A world that beckons
me to come

February 16, 2003

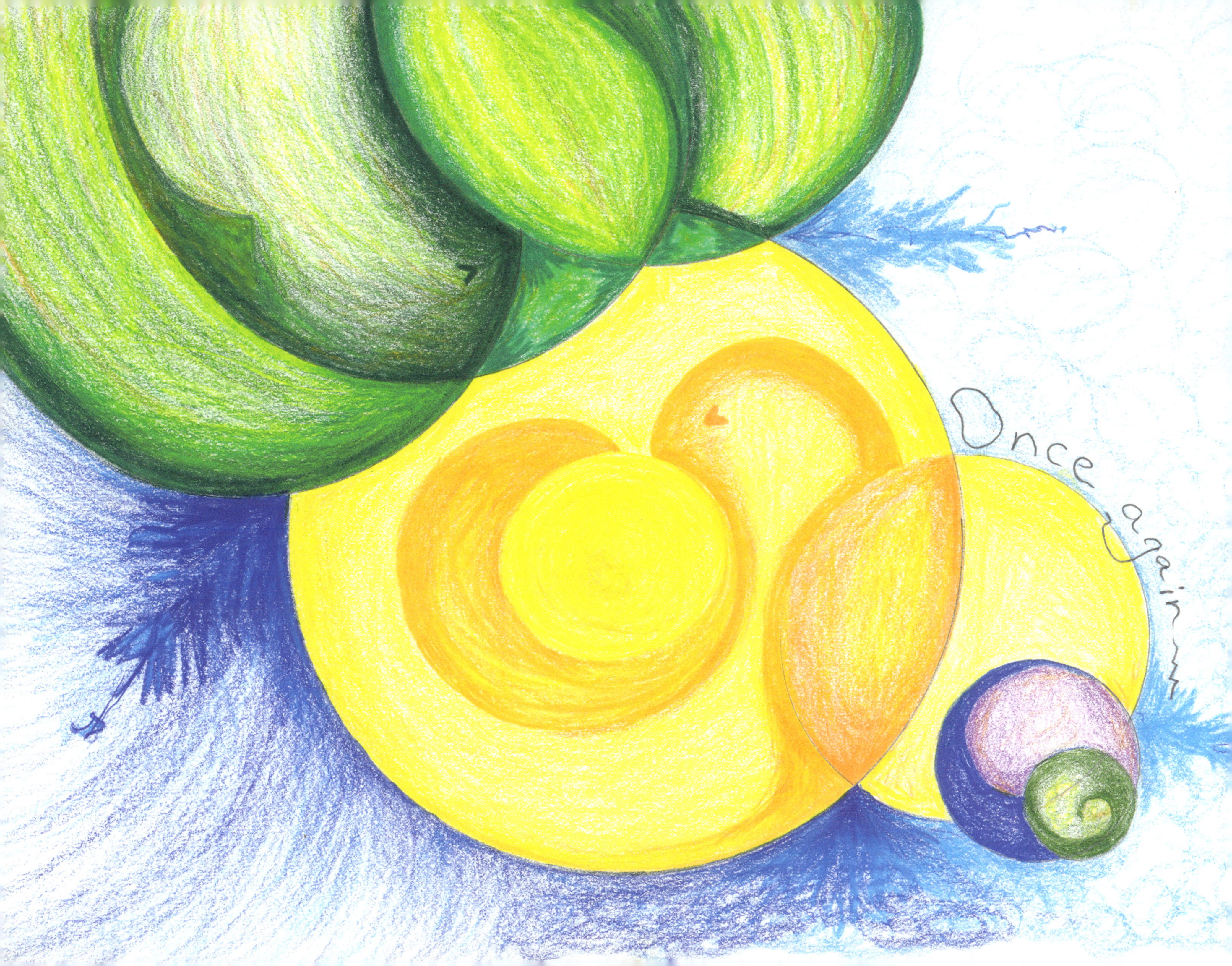
Once again

Waiting to be born in the fires of war...
Waiting
Waiting
To burst forth on the scene
And stand proudly on my ground
Green and rock solid beneath me
I need a green I can stand on
A rock to lay my head.

We're coming out now
To follow the vision that is born with us.

October 19, 2012

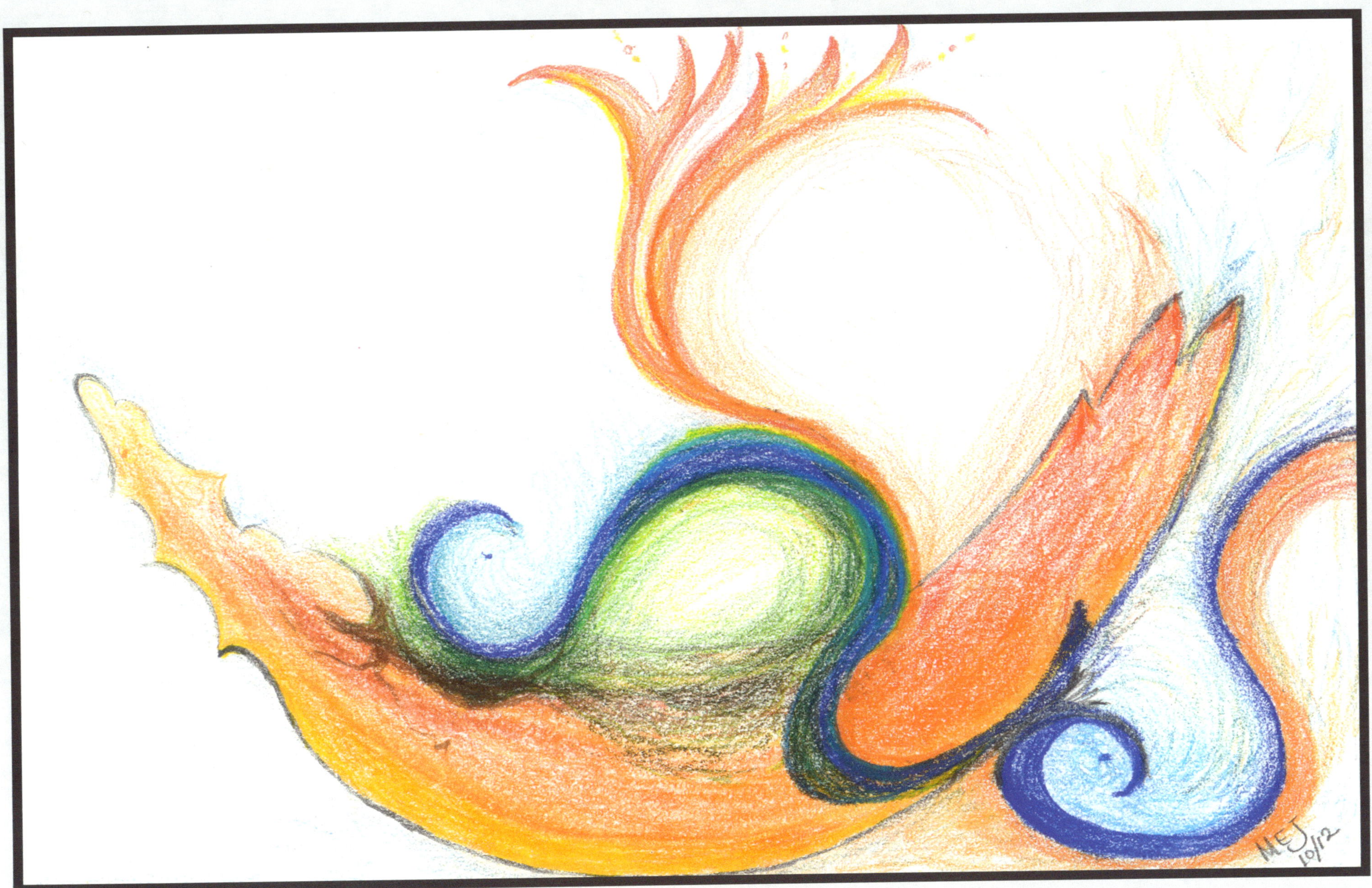

It's not time yet
    I'm still waiting
        So it must not be time yet.

NE ZAMAN? When?
    ŞIMDI   Now!
      ŞIMDI Now!

November 18, 2011

You could hear the gunshots
From the Island of Mytilene...

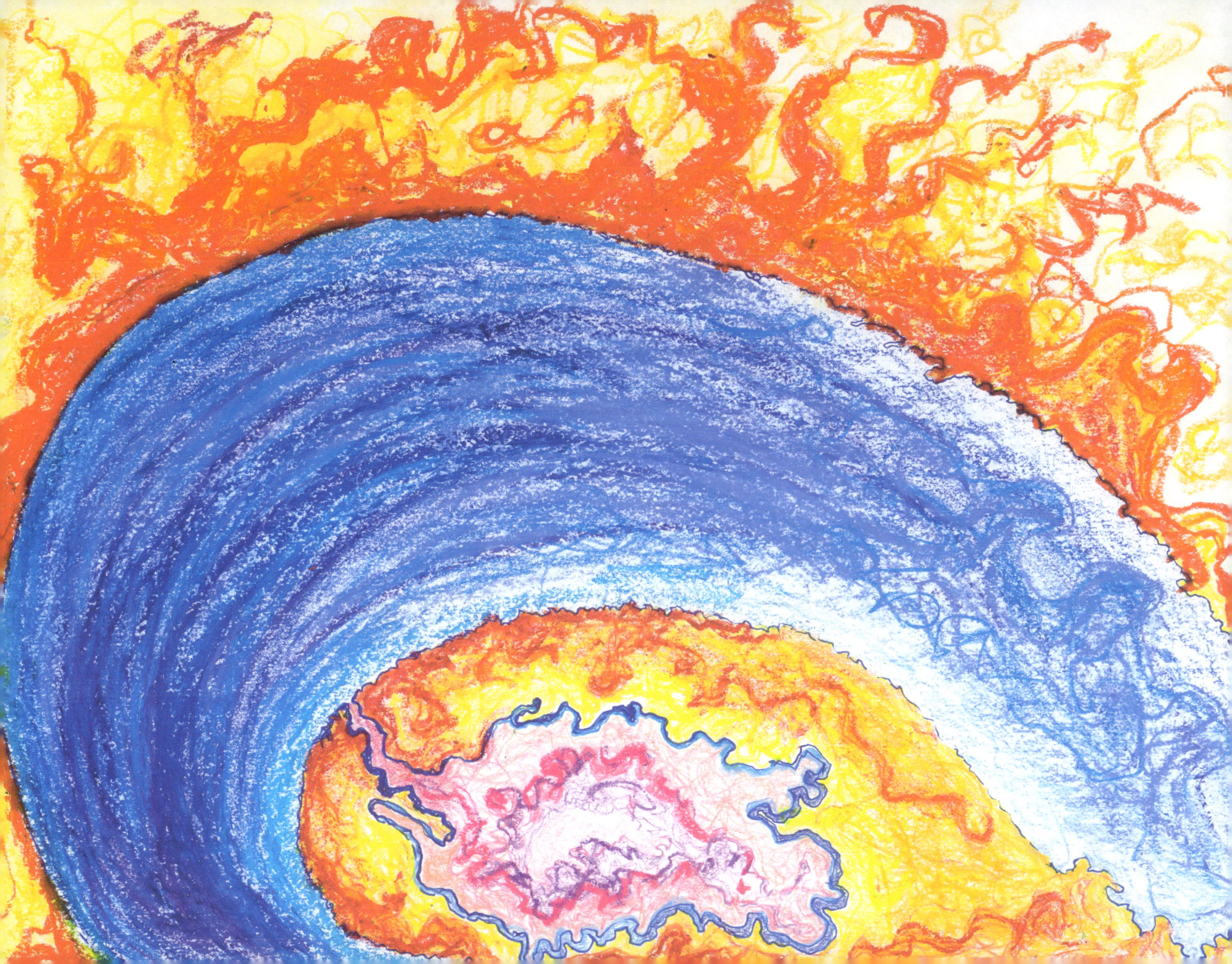

I want to come right up to your
edge and feel your warm skin
Wiggle my way inside of you
And wait...
until I am ready
To bloom
To dance
To sing
To be born.

October 14, 2011

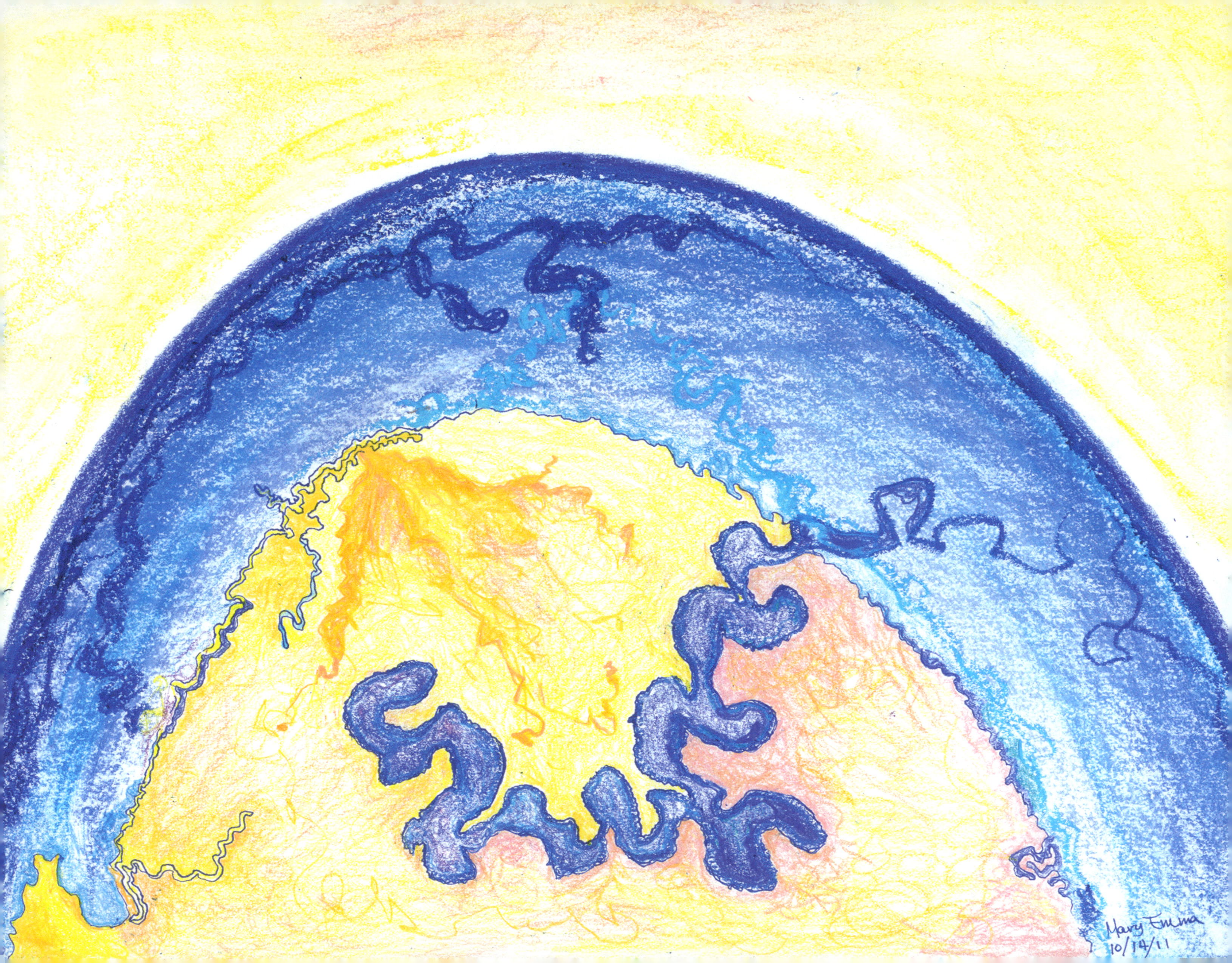

Mary Emma
10/14/11

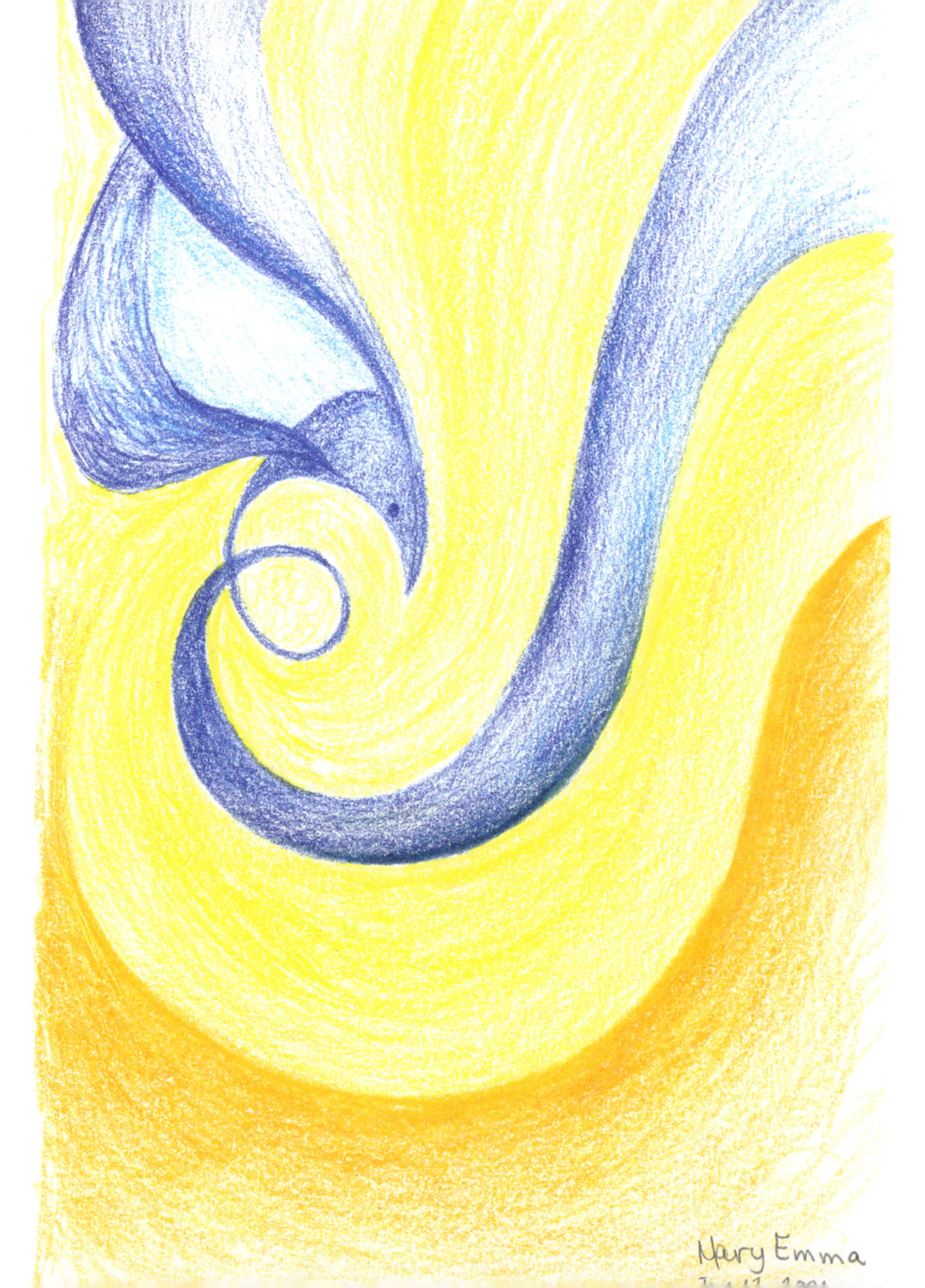
Mary Emma

Tumbling from another dimension
You plunge into my space
Bringing freedom and peace
We have always been connected
You and I
By a slender thread
Which often I could not see

January 12, 2001

My boat is sturdy and feels strong as it rocks gently
    on the sea of my memory
    on the sea of my life.

Past horror of war spoken in voices so soft I never
   heard them with my ears.
     The heart and the belly held the terror frozen from my mind until recent years
      Terror about learning something new
      Terror about arriving early
      Terror...

Now a witness is emerging
    A witness whose ears can hear the bombs
      whose eyes can glance quickly at
       the explosions on the island
        separated by space and time.

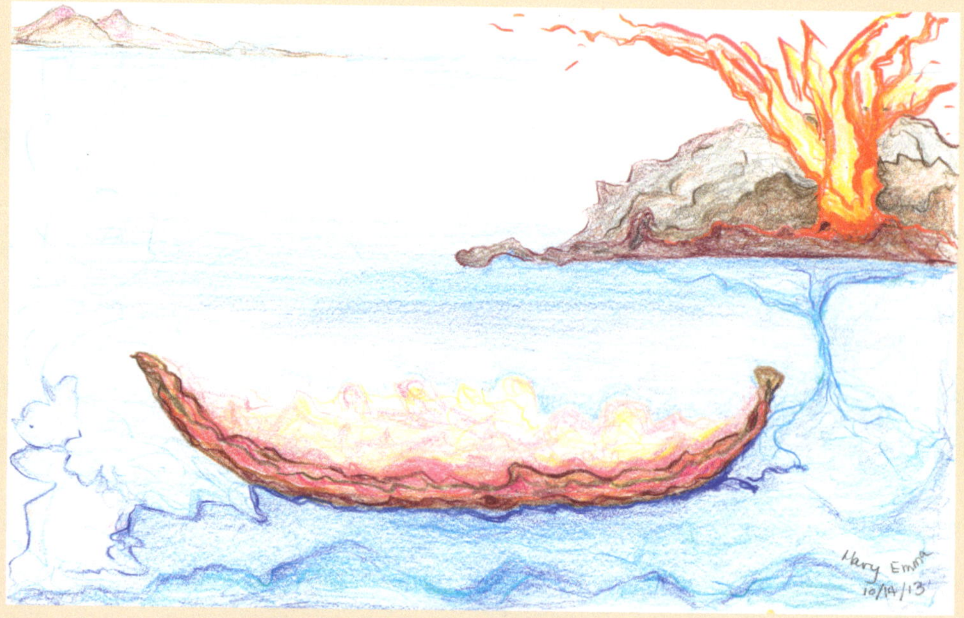

I rock gently in my sturdy boat and continue my journey into wholeness.

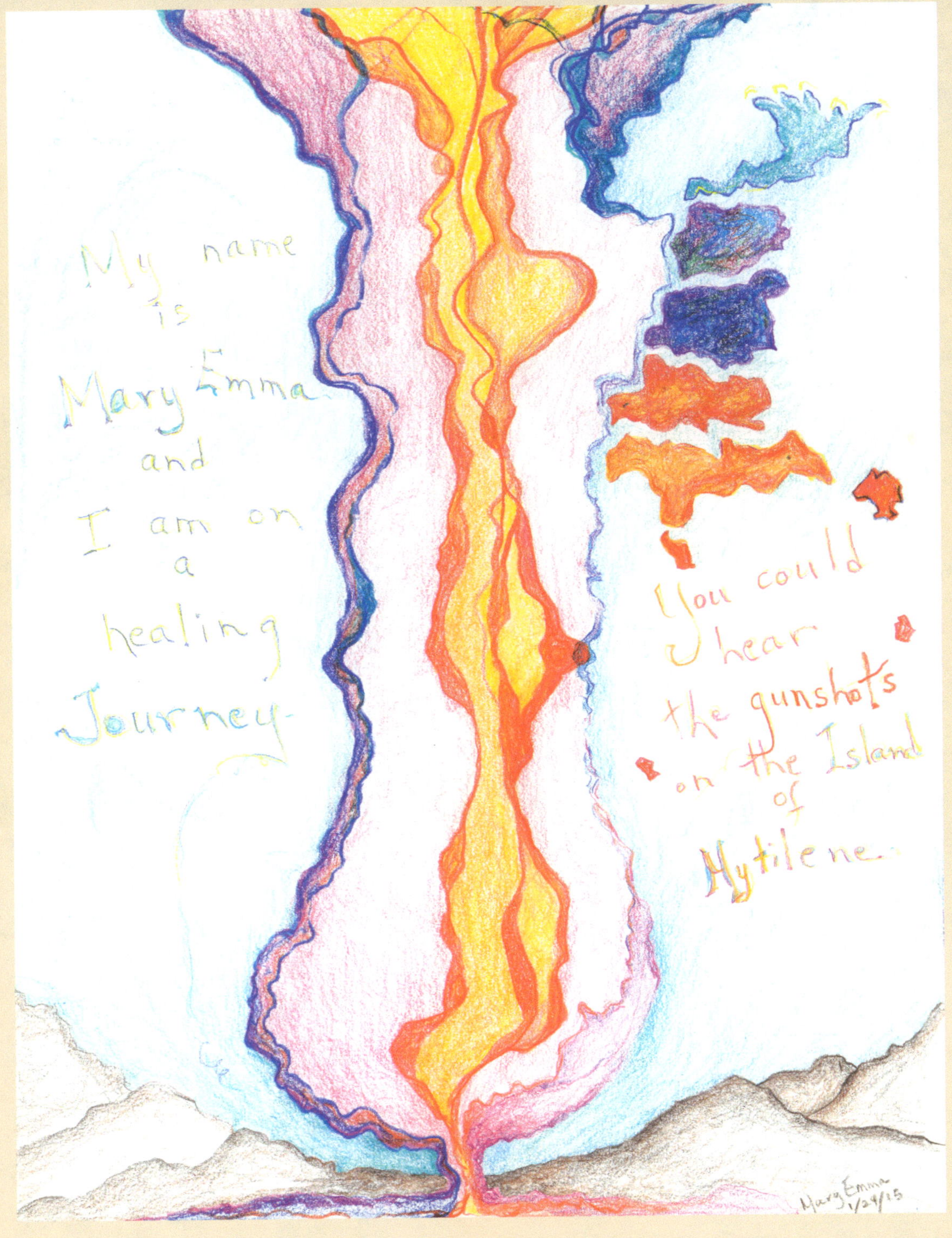

My name is Mary Emma and I am on a healing journey.

You could hear the gunshots on the Island of Mytilene.

January 24, 2015

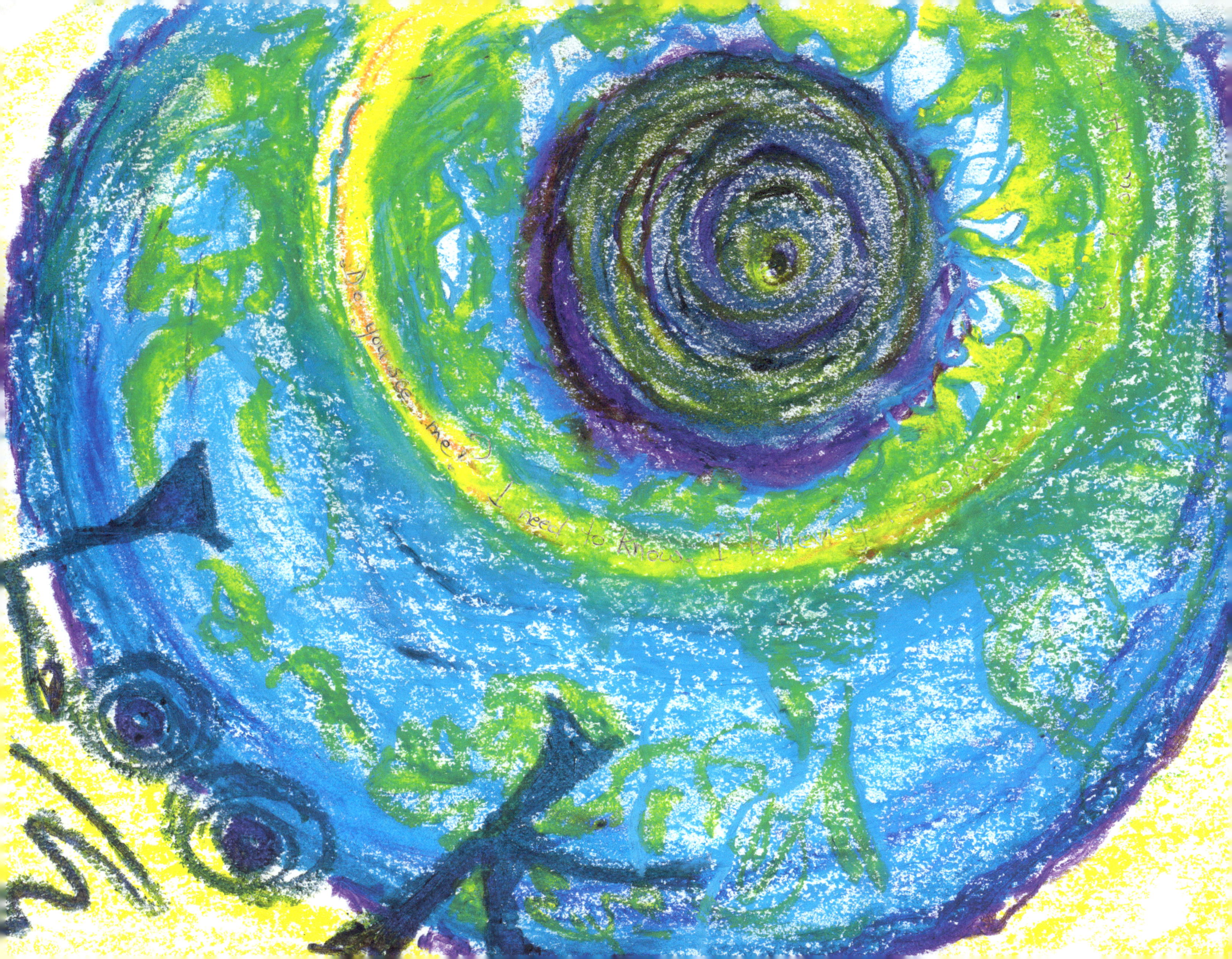

Do you see me? I need to know... I believe God sees me.

Look at me!
Do you see me?
I need to know!
I want to know!
I believe you saw me
You loved me
I know that.
You left me.
I wasn't ready
I needed you.
I didn't get to say good bye to you then.
I want to find a way to say good bye now

So LOOK at me!

9/27/11

My mother never liked pink...
And I tried to tell myself
She was right.
Pink was too feminine for a
Tomboy like me...

But sunsets and redbuds
Azaleas and peach blossoms
Continue to celebrate
Their pinkness and
Today I joined their party!

April 1, 2000

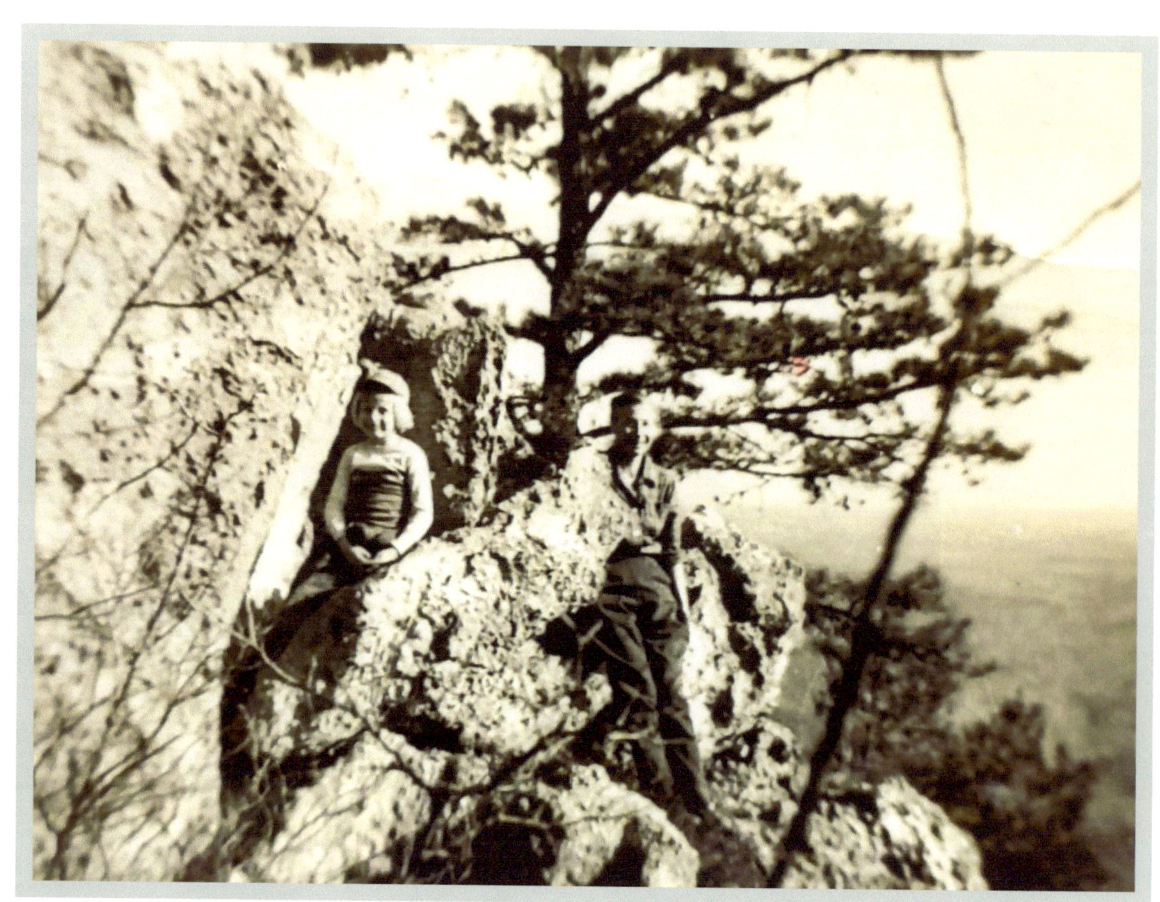

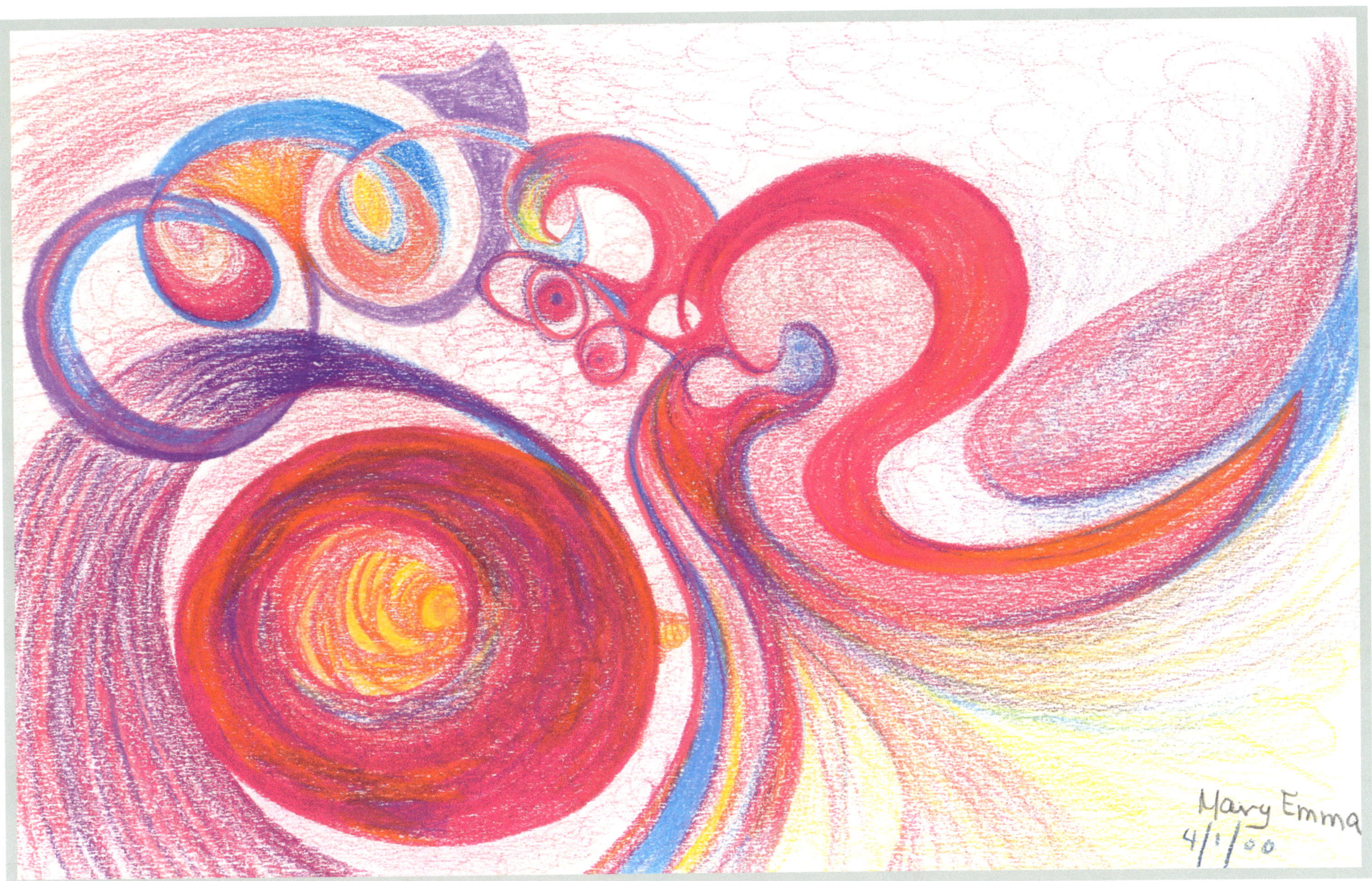

Mary Emma
4/1/00

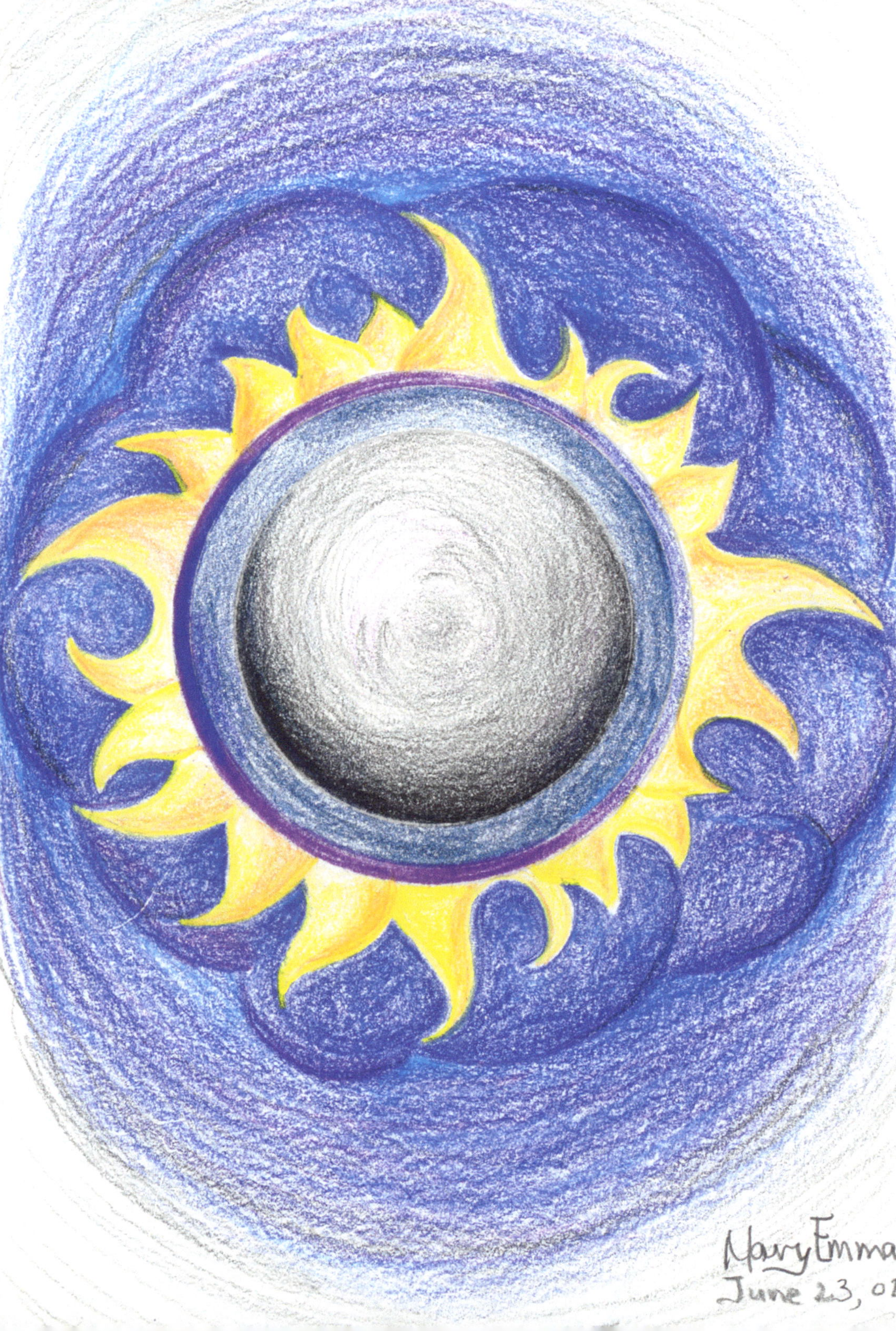

Fire...

I want to see your Love inside me
   Inside me...I want to see Your Light

Help me bring the light of your love to
   Myself and to the world

Mountains of ice at my core
   Crack open
      Slowly at first.

Tender shoots of life
   Creep through the crevices
   And burst into flower
      In the golden light of day.

November 4, 2011

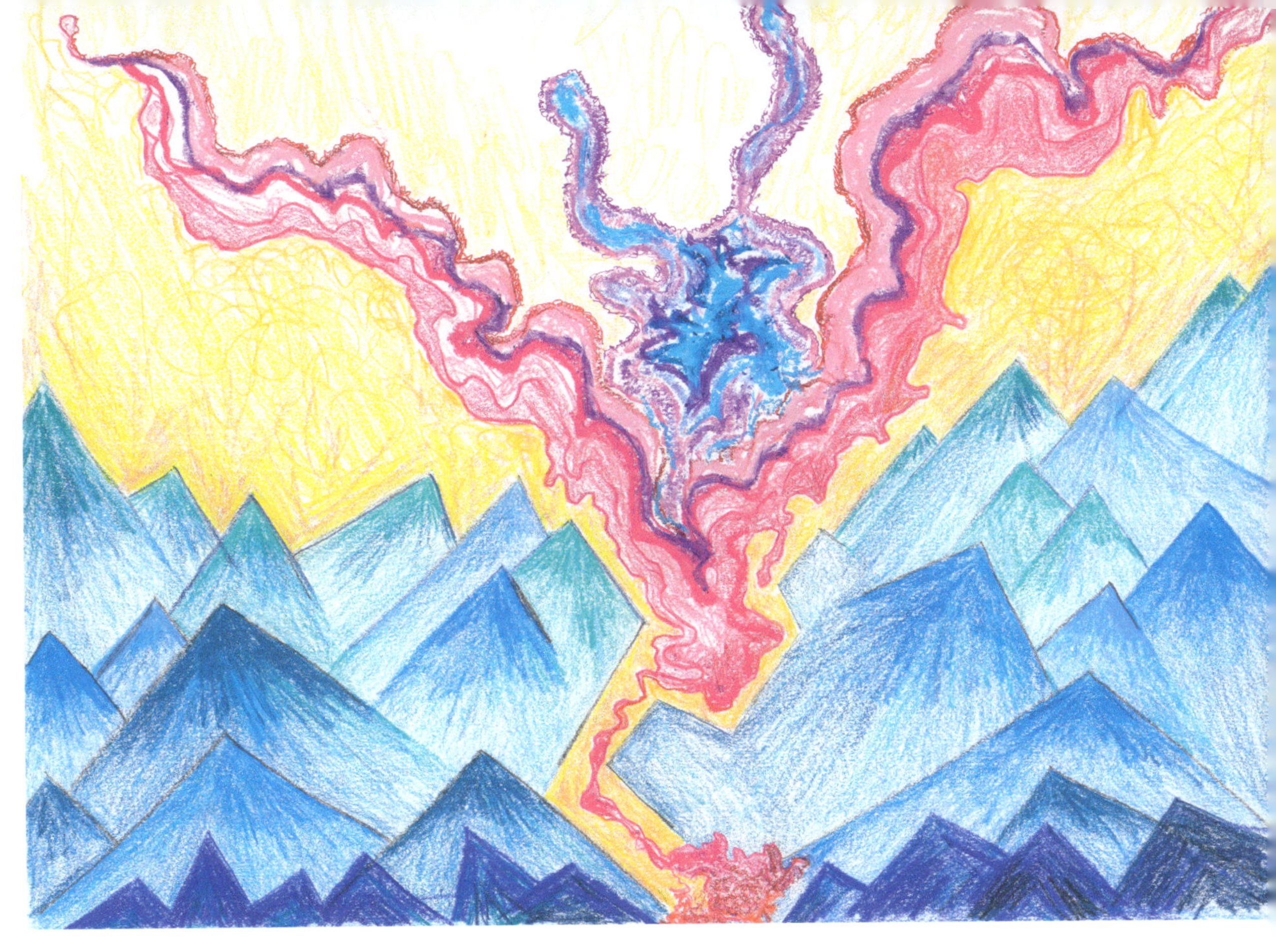

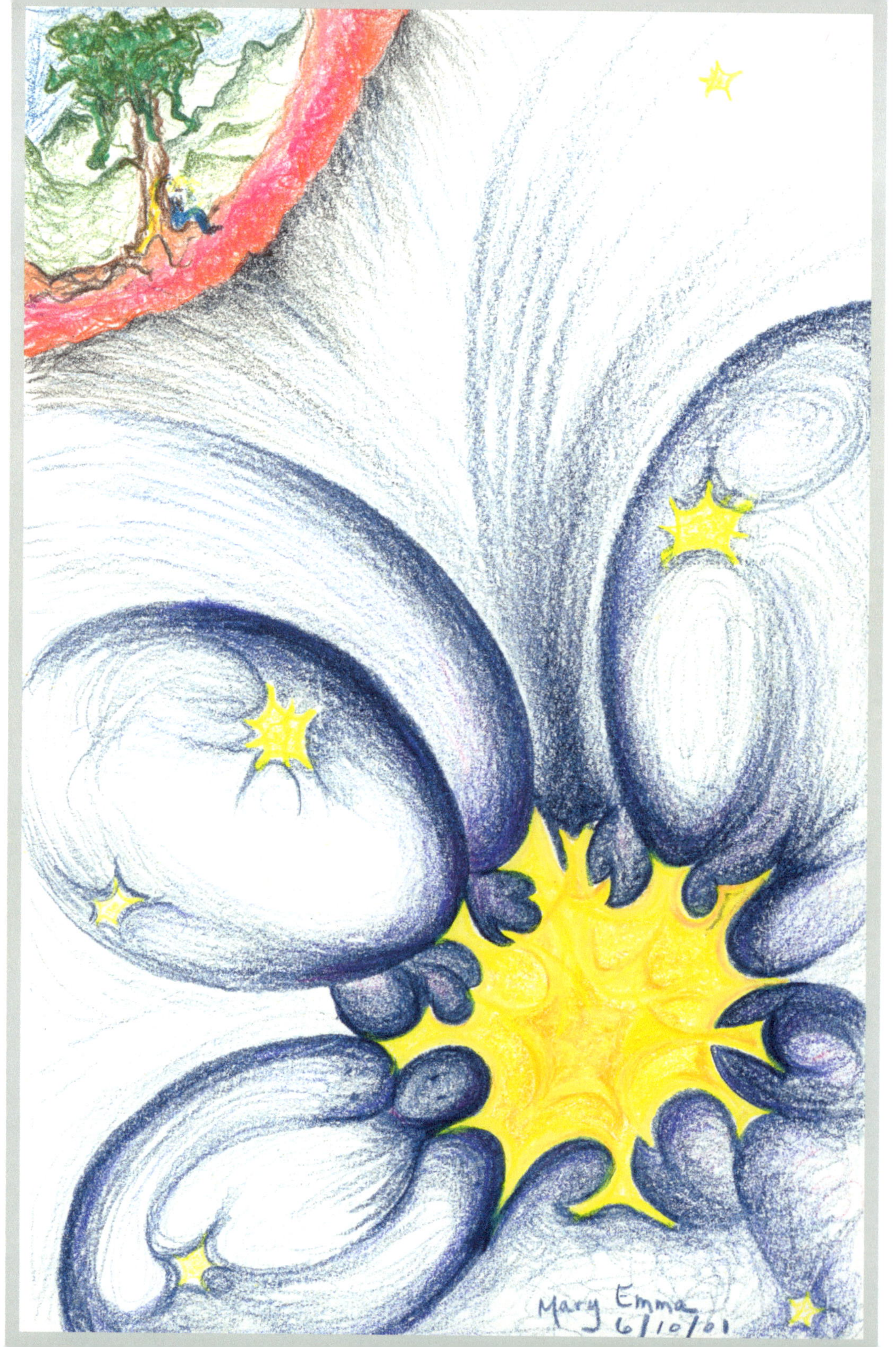

Mary Emma
6/10/01

Trees
I want to hear your voices in my
heart
Softly your branches caress my
space
Your still tall silence is my
mystery...
And yet in these afternoon
moments
I feel such peace
The space you create for me
Encloses me gently
So I wait...

June 10, 2001

I felt at home on that distant star,
I thought I'd stay awhile.
It was a tiny star and a brilliant one with
Gleaming golden points.
It was a tiny star
And so I shrunk to discover what I could.
As I grew smaller the landscape expanded before me
Into a gleaming golden desert
Surrounded by giant glimmering peaks.
I was so at home
And in quivering silence I waited.
The heavens were pulsating.
The air was alive.
Please stay, I heard.
Who are you, I wondered.
I am your Joy. I am your Life.
I am your Self.
I want to embrace you, the Voice said.
In quivering silence, I melted
Into the invisible arms and wept.

February 2001

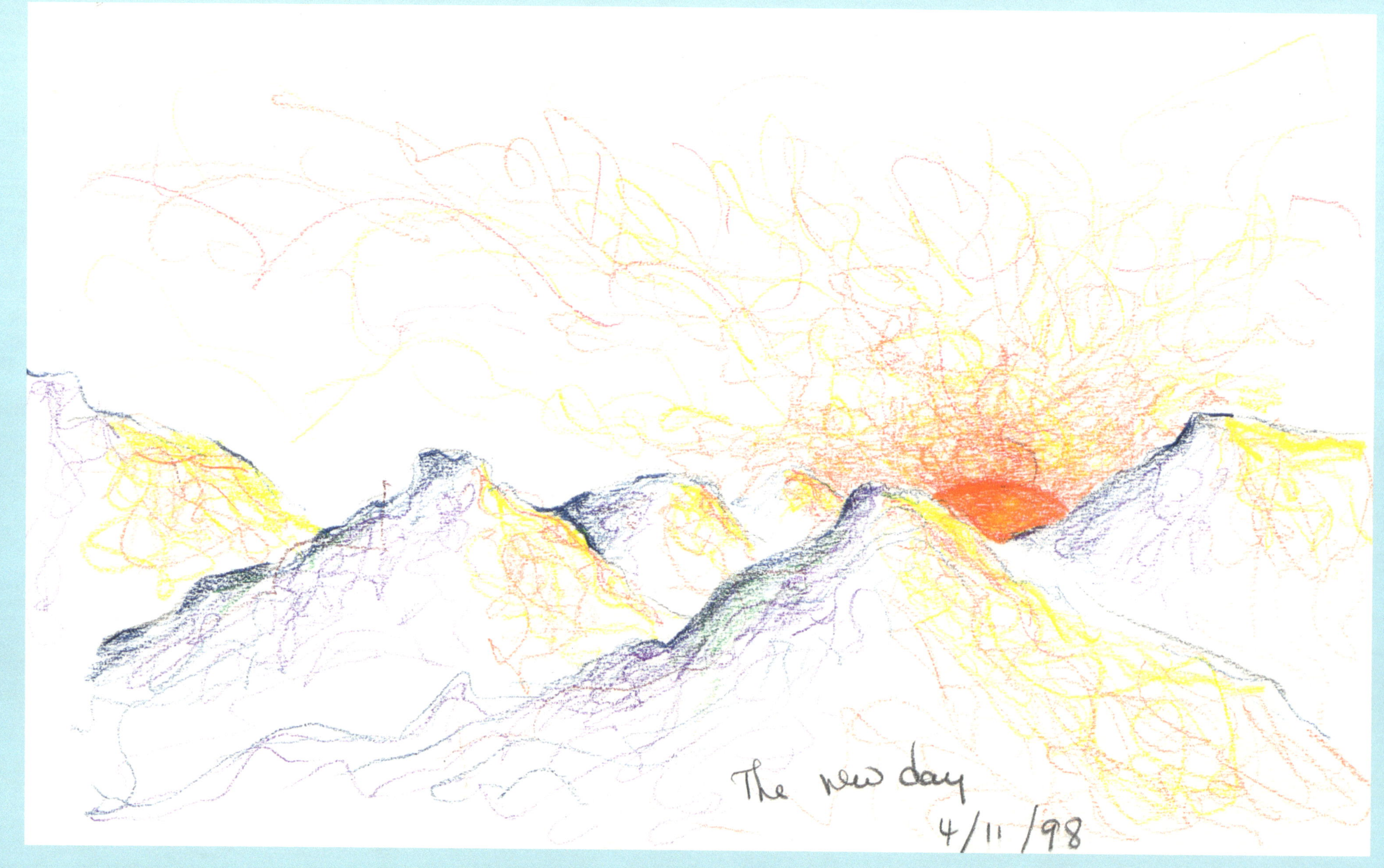

The new day ...

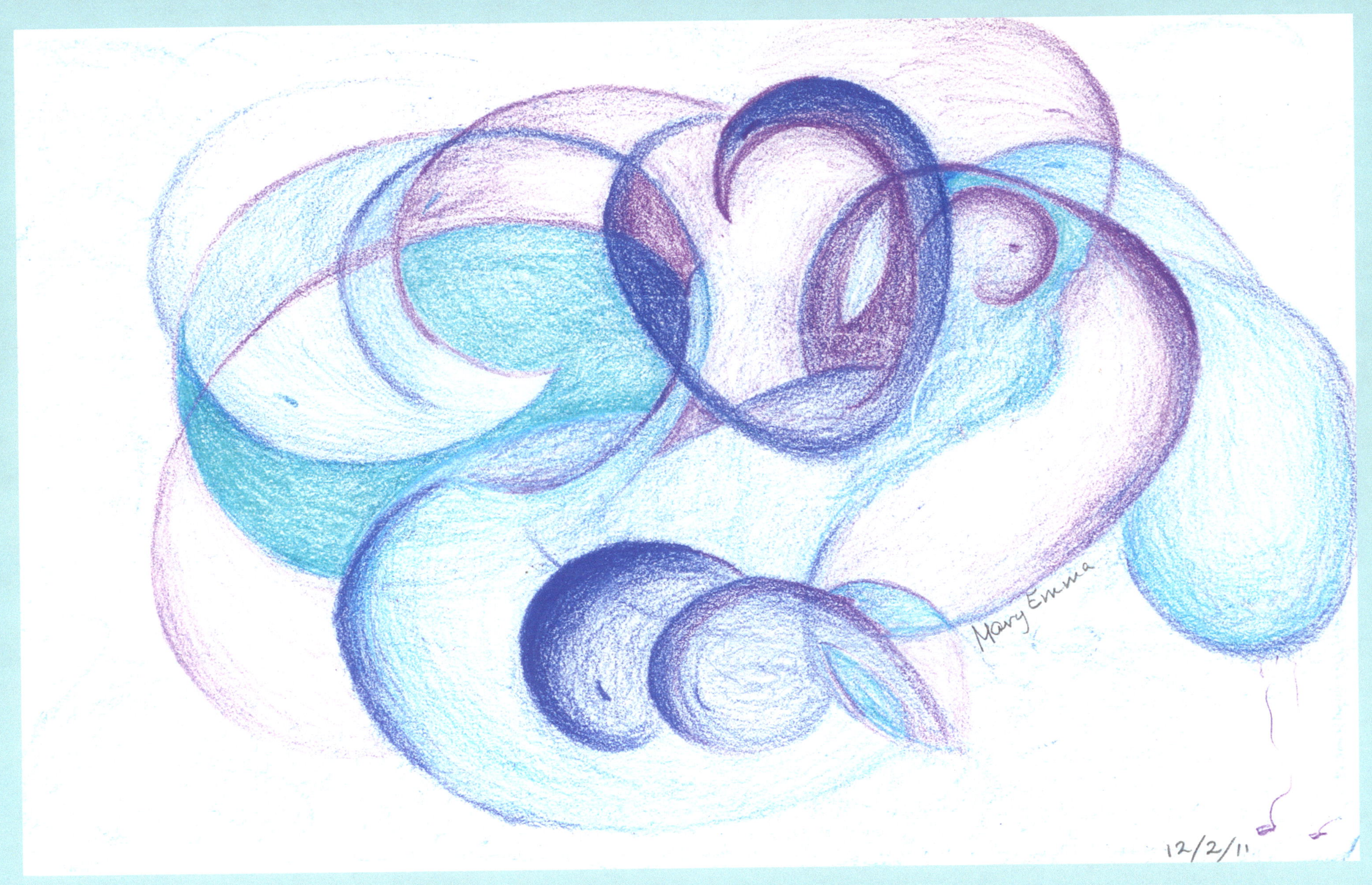

... *Blue circles resting down.*

I wondered what had happened to that time we had
together
    . . . on that hill top looking down
        Onto the fishing boats
        In the Black Sea
    . . . under the domes of
        Aya Sophia, Sulelymaniye
        And the Blue Mosque
    . . . along bustling
        Narrow streets leading from
        Kapili Carsi to the Spice Bazaar
    . . . on the ferry crossing
        The Marmaris in the black of night
        As we made our way to Izmir
    . . . on the hilltop of
        Ancient ruins looking
        Out to the islands in the Aegean
    . . . on the coast of the
        Mediterranean when the peaceful blue waters
        of Oludeniz
        Brought us rest...

What happened to the way we were together on our
journey to the East?...

Consumed on our return
    . . . by the demands of a new and growing practice
    . . . by the pressures of the job search
    . . . by the daily routine

Today we came to the
Woods to be together
In this sacred space

And sitting on the
side of the mountain
on Sunset Ridge
Overlooking Young Harris and
Brasstown Valley
I feel that I have
returned to that
time we spent
together in that land so far away

October 21, 1998

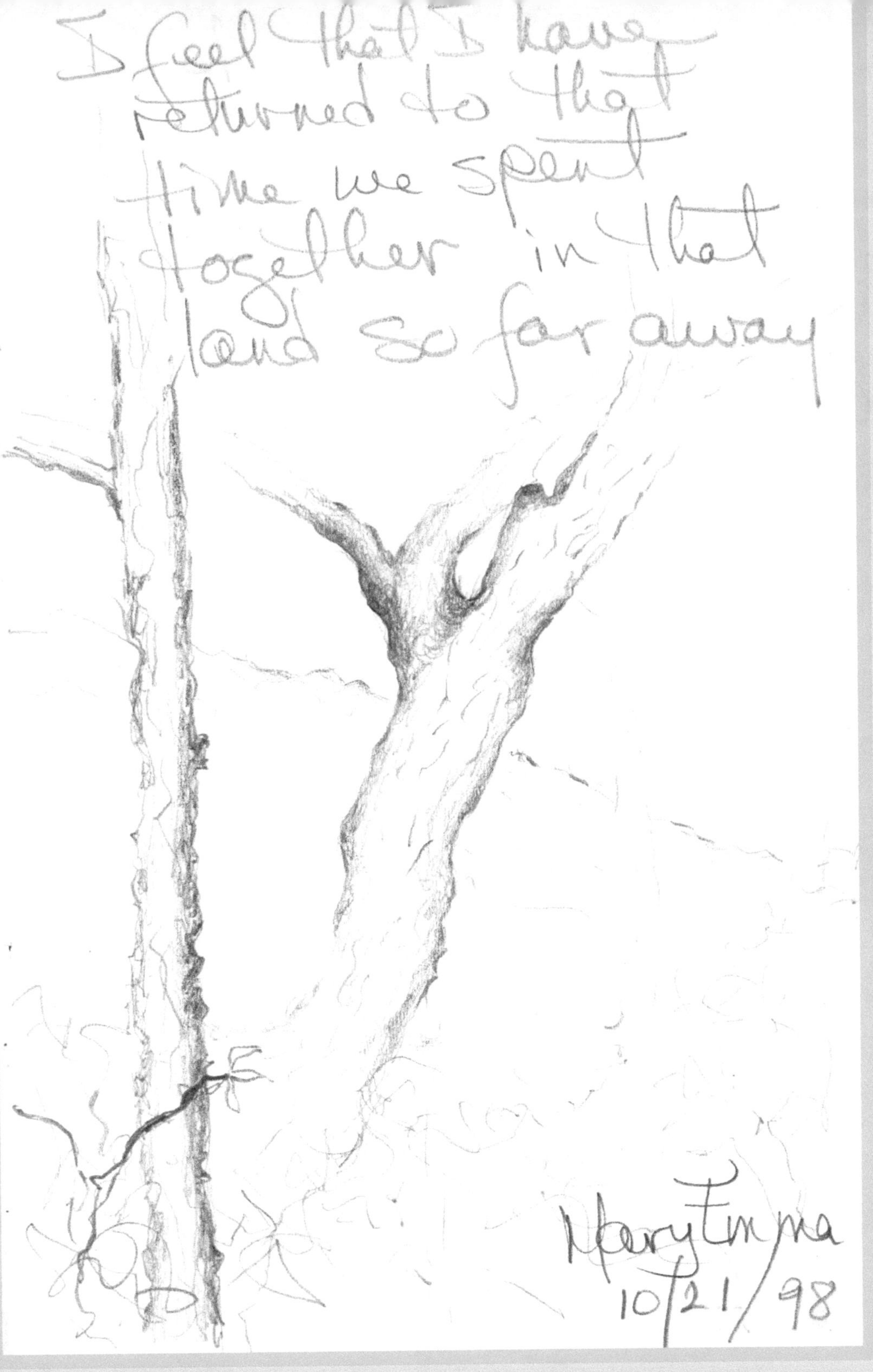

I feel that I have
returned to that
time we spent
together in that
land so far away

MaryEmma
10/21/98

Garden of the Soul, Garden of the Self
A place where the universe resides.
When you are there and I am there,
Then we are one.
Namaste